MW00490906

Food and God

Food and God

A Theological Approach to Eating, Diet, and Weight Control

JOEL R. SOZA

WIPF & STOCK · Eugene, Oregon

FOOD AND GOD
A Theological Approach to Eating, Diet, and Weight Control

Wipf & Stock
A Division of Wipf and Stock Publishers
199 W. 8th Ave., Suite 3
Eugene, OR 97401
www.wipfandstock.com

ISBN 13: 978-1-60608-224-9

Manufactured in the U.S.A.

Dedicated to Joseph and Shari,
my children and my most precious gifts from God.
May you enjoy a long, healthy life
and many "H" days.

Contents

Introduction ix

1 FOOD AND THE BEGINNING OF GOD'S REVELATION 1

The role of food and eating in creation
The role of food and eating in temptation
Points to ponder

2 FOOD AND EATING IN ANCIENT ISRAEL 11

The role of labor in everyday life food preparation
The role of food and eating in Israel's law code
Points to ponder

3 FOOD AND THE WISDOM OF SAGES 23

Gluttony
Old Testament case studies: Esau, Eglon, and Eli
Points to ponder

4 FOOD AND EATING IN THE LIFE AND TEACHING
OF JESUS 48

The synoptic gospels
The gospel of John
Points to ponder

5 FOOD AND EATING IN THE NEW TESTAMENT
CHURCH 68

Food, fellowship, and the Gentile mission
The Lord's Supper
Points to ponder

Summary: Digesting It All 89
Appendix: The Ten Commandments of Eating 101
Bibliography 105

Introduction

"FOOD, GLORIOUS food" is how I remember it. This line rang out in the opening song of the movie I was watching. It was the musical version of Charles Dickens's classic mid-nineteenth-century tale *Oliver Twist*. Scores of young boys performed their song-and-dance routine in their work-house, orphanage environment longing to know what life would be like if they were able to grow fat, indulging in every assortment of food one could imagine. For most Americans today, this is not the problem. Instead, the concern is growing skinny, or at least trying to avoid the numerous quantities of food that surround us on every side and cause us as a nation to grow fat and unhealthy.

Besides the obvious weight problem and food obsession America has, which is clear from casual observation of physiques and body shapes in just about any public setting, there were numerous other promptings over time that also became an impetus for writing this book. For instance, while recently attempting to watch a film in a public theater, I found myself enormously distracted by a constant and consistent crunching sound coming from the back row. I turned my head just enough on a few occasions in a desperate, yet failed, attempt to alert the middle-aged husband and wife to the distraction they were causing as a result of perhaps "over-enjoying" their popcorn. In a similar fashion, I recall taking in the sights, sounds, and smells of a Major League Baseball stadium some years ago only to find that what fascinated me most was not the slow-moving game, but rather the meticulous devouring by a young man of what surely must have been every available food item for sale in the stadium. I was sickened by both the expense he put out and the grease, calories, and cholesterol he put in.

On another occasion, I boarded a fairly unoccupied airplane for a cross-nation trip, only to discover, to my dismay, that my row and seat number landed me smack in between two very large and obese women of a particular religious order who each took up the space of one-and-a-half seats. Upon discovering that my much smaller frame was going in the seat between them, of which there was virtually nothing left, they looked me up and down as if to insinuate how rude it was of me to take the seat that I of course paid for, but which was basically now non-existent.

Speaking of airplanes, the numerous cross-Atlantic flights I had to take while studying in graduate school also afforded me the opportunity to witness firsthand the food and eating crisis that is very real in America and other Western nations as well. The movies provided some entertainment to pass the time, but I was more amused watching the flight attendants move from one task to the next to meet the demands of the passengers, each of which had to do with food and drink. I remember thinking to myself that continual filling of bowel and bladder of a few hundred people during eight hours of close-quarters inactivity thousands of feet above the surface of the earth was probably not such a good idea. Were we really that hungry? Although not aerodynamically trained, I began to calculate in my head what the load limit might be for the airplane and whether we had surpassed capacity since we started the trip. One television commercial recently advertised a fast-food product by applauding a man for boarding an airplane, in between two pretty women incidentally, with his extra-large, fully loaded grease burger and accessories, and the women, of course, as a consequence were drawn to the man and his meal. Does having the contents of an overstuffed burger falling on one's lap get the attention of pretty women for a man? Would a person really board an airplane eating this way?

Ironically, I experienced this very thing after having penned these words. A man sat next to me on an airplane, having brought with him an extra-large burger and fries. He consumed it all before takeoff. All that was missing was the pretty women escorting him. Although eating like this would be the furthest thing from my mind in such a context, it may be more and more the norm for Americans. In fact, a recent television program discussed a "growing" (pun intended) problem the airline industry is encountering because the passenger weight average is increasing so much that customers may eventually have to purchase a ticket priced on their weight. Corporate America in general, as well as the public school and health care systems, are all facing serious issues in regard to America's over-indulgence in food and Americans' resulting weight problems. There has even been talk of a "fat tax," which would raise the expense of non-nutritional fatty foods similar to extra taxes added to health risk items like tobacco and alcohol.

In a word, the thesis of this book is to challenge and provide a solution to America and the Christian Church in America in regard to food over-indulgence. If there is one statement to remember long after this book has been read, it would be, *"Think before you eat!"* This book attempts to get one to think theologically about food. Food is a provision from God and should be thought of as such every time consumption occurs. There are numerous good books about food that approach the topic from every conceivable viewpoint.[1] There are socio-cultural approaches, environmental approaches, nutritional and health approaches, aesthetic approaches, and that which moves most in a theological direction, ethical approaches. All of these provide invaluable insight into the way we go about purchasing, preparing, and con-

---

1. Some recent titles include: Buford, *Heat;* Belasco, *Meals to Come;* Pollan, *In Defense of Food;* Pollan, *The Omnivore's Dilemma*; Mason and Singer, *The Way We Eat*; Nestle, *What to Eat.*

suming food, some of which have genuine theological concerns.[2] But this book is not one of those kinds of books, for all these approaches are ultimately inadequate in and of themselves. Instead, a theological understanding of food, based on a proper and systematic biblical foundation, is what America and the Christian Church in America need to consider in regard to this issue. This book is theological. By "theological," I simply mean the logic of God on the topic from the standpoint of the Christian tradition.[3] I am trying to explore what the nature, character, and thought of God, as ascertained from Scripture, might be when it comes to humans eating food.

Psychologists, anthropologists, naturalists, nutritionists, medical professionals, and even politicians are all beginning to have a say regarding the American fat and food epidemic. These are all helpful and necessary voices.[4] But what is mostly needed

2. I have found Michael Pollan's book *In Defense of Food: An Eater's Manifesto* especially helpful. Pollan's three-fold thesis is: eat food, not too much, mostly plants. By "eat food," he means avoiding processed and packaged foods and eating those natural items that could truly be called "food." The "not too much" and "mostly plants" is self-explanatory.

3. Theology as a term has its root in two Greek words: Theos = "God," and Logos = "Logic/Study"; literally, "the logic of God."

4. Halliday and Halliday, *Thin Again,* 11. For instance, Judy and Arthur Halliday, an RN and MD respectively, wrote a book with a similar title to this one. Their basic premise is that overwhelming food urges are really the manifestation of a deeper need, what they call "the silent hunger of the starving soul." The book offers a useful contribution in contending that we all hunger for God and that only in Christ can this hunger be satisfied. The medical couple provides story after story of people used and abused who must reckon with the great possibility that their inordinate love of food is masking deeper problems within the complexity of the human self. They provide a biblical and evangelical approach to the problem, something with which this author is in full agreement. However, their book, written from the standpoint of medical training, does not have the benefit of being written with a carefully trained theological and exegetical eye. Therefore, although the Hallidays'

is the prophetic voice of Scripture to call a nation to re-think that which it takes for granted. Israel's prophets of antiquity in the Old Testament called for a nation to repent because of a variety of self-indulgent sins. Interestingly enough, sometimes judgment was to be exacted through a cutting off of Israel's/Judah's food supply (e.g., Amos 4:6 and Joel 1) as they had been forewarned (Deut 28:17). Stated quite simply today, America and the Christian Church therein are in need of theological renewal in the area of food and eating. A less-sophisticated way to express it is to say "repent," which simply means to turn around and go in a different direction. It is the hope of this book that in bringing people back to God (the source of all food and life) in the matter of food and eating through a well-thought out, orderly approach revealed in Scripture, vibrant physical, emotional, and spiritual life can be restored to individuals and even family units.

Before progressing further, it should be made clear that the aforementioned anecdotes and expressions are not coming from a soul who thinks he is not in need of renewal in this area, whereas almost everyone else is. In fact, *the* leading purpose in carrying out this study was because the author became very displeased with his own approach to food. Although only pesky portions of fat appear on my body from time to time, thanks in no small part to a good metabolism and smaller-stature genetics, I found myself consistently hoarding and gulping my food, without much regard for what I was eating, how much I was eating, and the time frame it took to eat it. As I aged, I began to notice certain gastronomic phenomena. Most obvious were those things resulting from a case of esophagitus and acid reflux. I needed to change my eating habits, and I needed to do it immediately. I ate too much non-life-giving foods, too fast, and with too little thought. I was really not that much different than those with obvious weight problems, and I needed to take a long,

book is similar in title, theme, and concern to this book, it is not able to cover the same kind of ground.

hard look at myself in this area. Perhaps I should have picked up clues from long ago, such as when a college roommate accused me of "mantling" my food.[5] This book is simply my own pilgrimage through an area I want to improve upon in my life spiritually, physically, and psychologically. I can only hope that I am changed for the better, and that somehow, you, the reader, will come on the journey with me also to be changed and to develop a theological approach to food, diet, and weight control.

I dedicate this book to my precious wife, Migdalia, and my beautiful children, Joseph and Shari. It was Joseph, who, at the tender age of ten, brainstormed a new family tradition, a few days each year called "H" days. These days would be devoted to physical *health*, hence the designation "H." The family would spend the day eating healthy foods only, drinking water, playing games, and exercising. This created a greater awareness in us of our need for the deliberate practice of good health habits in our daily routines. As I said in my earlier dedication, may the four of us enjoy many "H" days together and long lives filled with thankfulness to our Lord Jesus Christ for his provision of food. I am especially grateful to Malone University for granting me a sabbatical during the fall term of 2007 so that I might devote myself to this project. It is my hope that this book will reflect the excellence that the Malone family consistently demonstrates.

5. Thanks, Lenny.

Food and the Beginning of God's Revelation

IT IS significant to note that food and eating play an important role in the opening pages of the Bible. This chapter will focus on the role of food and eating in two of the most critical and discussed narratives within the early Bible story: creation and temptation.

THE ROLE OF FOOD AND EATING IN CREATION

The biblical creation account as recorded in Genesis 1 and 2 has long been a topic of great interest and debate. Chapter 1 in particular paints the picture of God's creative work with a broad brushstroke, leaving out many possible details that we the readers would love to have access to but simply do not. Basically, Genesis 1 is not written to answer all of our how questions but rather to provide an answer to the who question. The God of Israel alone is God, and he alone is creator of all. The point is obvious and direct. Yet there are a few details given that, when carefully considered, provide valuable insight into the nature of God. There is a point of detail about the third day provided that uses selective word choice to indicate that God had already prepared in advance for humankind's need for food. This is seen in 1:11–12 where vegetation is mentioned, but only such kind as afforded by the Hebrew word that indicates food-producing vegetation.

> Then God said, "Let the earth put forth vegetation: plants yielding seed, and fruit trees of every kind on earth that bear fruit with the seed in it." And it was so. The earth brought forth vegetation: plants yielding seed of every kind, and trees of every kind bearing fruit with the seed in it. And God saw that it was good (Gen 1:11–12).

God was not merely creating the earth; he was already furnishing it with food for living beings that had not yet been created. Food was not an afterthought! He furnished the earth with the necessary vegetation, as he would also do in the Garden of Eden (Gen 2:8–9).

In order to prepare the earth for its task, however, God first had to separate the dry ground from the waters, which had fully covered the earth (Gen 1:2). The Ancient Near Eastern world is replete with stories of watery chaos. There are numerous flood accounts, some of which parallel the Noah flood, and many of which indicate that the so-called gods of the ancient world were incapable of controlling the waters. Genesis 1 demonstrates, however, that the God of Israel does not find the powerful waters to be problematic to control. In fact, he is in perfect control as he simply speaks the word to separate out the waters from the dry land (Gen 1:6–10). It is well attested that the Israelites themselves were a people who had great fear and respect for the sea and were not a naturally sea-going people. The sea represented for them, as for other ancient peoples, a place of mystery, intrigue, and chaos, which is likely some of the background behind the Leviathan creature of Job, who probably represents that which Israel fears the most in life (Job 41:1). Many of us have similar trepidations when it comes to venturing into the sea. I for one am content to wade in waist-deep off the beach, but as soon as I sense I can no longer see what might lurk below or move fast enough to get out of the water, I begin to retreat toward land. The point is, the power of water, be it the mighty seas or the terror of flood, continues to hold a place in the imagination of many as that which is to be avoided and feared. In fact, some of the most important parts of the grand narrative that follows throughout the Old Testament are the devastating flood of Genesis 6 through 8 and the miraculous crossing of the Red Sea (Exod 14). In both places, God is in control of the mighty waters. This transcends into the New Testament accounts of Jesus walking on water (Mark 6:45–52) and calming the sea (Mark 4:35–41). In so doing, Jesus demonstrated himself to be God.

We should know, then, that the portrait of God easily distinguishing dry land from the waters in early Genesis is a statement of his greatness, and all the more so because he has in effect "set the table" for humankind to be able to eat the food of the dry land, something that could not have happened if God were incapable of setting apart the water from the land. Therefore, the dry land and its ability to produce food is a gift from God! It is interesting to note that the sea does not produce fish to eat, in the sense of "growing fish," nor does the sky produce birds, in the sense of "growing birds," to eat, but the land is special; it can produce crops and vegetation and as such should be well attended and cared for. The Hebrew word for ground is a feminine noun,[1] so perhaps the concept of a "mother-earth" is not that farfetched after all, as long as it supersedes a humanistic concept that does not give ultimate glory to the creator God, who in his provision and care made the earth to be a life-sustaining force. Those who would remind us of a responsible ecology in doing theology provide a necessary service for us all. Some traditions of Jewish synagogues and prayer books have included a prayer of thanksgiving for meals along the lines of "Blessed art Thou, Lord our God, King of the world, who causes

---

1. Pronounced *adamah*, which, as one might discern, is related to the first man's name, Adam, because he was made from the ground. This reinforces humankind's connectedness with the land. As the food that keeps us alive comes from the ground, so also the origin of our life has come from the same ground.

to come forth bread from the earth."[2] This is a prayer worth incorporating into our personal lives.

The creation account includes other facets of God's handiwork, of course, such as the creation of sun, moon, stars, birds, fish, mammals, and humans. The climax of creation is clearly humans, whom God has fashioned after his own image (Gen 1:26–27) and given other life forms to rule over (Gen 1:28). Interestingly enough, the continuation of the narrative in verse 29 returns back to a theme of the third day, which is vegetation, this time with the particular mention of its usefulness as food. The animals are also given food (v. 30), but it is a slightly different word in the Hebrew. This suggests that the food preparation of the third day was for humankind only, implying that human beings were indeed foremost in God's great creative plan and that a food supply was foremost for human provision. Simply stated, the creation of humans and food holds a significant place at the very beginning of God's grand narrative.

Ancient Mesopotamian accounts of human origins depict a worldview where humans are created to serve the gods and supply them with food. Genesis 1 contradicts this notion, putting forward in clear terms that the one true God did not create human beings to be his slaves, nor are they expected to supply him with food. Instead, thankfully, it is the opposite; God created human beings special, in his very image, and he has provided food for them before they even existed. It is likely that the ancient Israelites at times confused their God with the influences of surrounding pantheons in this matter. For instance, the prophet Micah, living some seven hundred years before Christ, challenged the Israelites about their thinking that the animal sacrifices they brought to the temple were to satisfy God's hunger. They may have been perplexed at his seemingly endless appetite as he devoured up to "thousands of rams" (Mic 6:7) in one sitting and yet was not satisfied. Micah sets the record straight by

2. Gower, *The New Manners And Customs Of Bible Times*, 54.

putting forth what really satisfies God's hunger, which is "to do justice, love kindness, and walk humbly with God" (Mic 6:8).

Next time, if ever, we feel hunger pangs, perhaps we should think about what causes God to feel, metaphorically speaking, hunger pangs. This important text from Micah alone is enough to get one thinking theologically about food. God hungers for a certain kind of human action that has the interest of what is right in mind. Our natural desire for food should be overshadowed by a greater desire to see a society and culture that has the practice of justice, kindness, and humility at the forefront. Tom P. Hafer, in his book *Faith & Fitness (Diet and Exercise for a Better World)*, has put forth a thesis that Americans need to transform their thinking from a "need to lose weight" mentality, to a "need to feed" mentality.[3] Rather than changing our eating habits merely for ourselves, we should gain awareness of the problem of global hunger and demonstrate such awareness by our own streamlined and responsible eating habits. This is the kind of human action God hungers for: a justice, kindness, and humility that we can put into practice every day by the choices we make when we eat. Hafer's book is quite useful in spelling out some practical ways that we can practice a "need to feed" lifestyle.

Genesis 2 puts forth a creation account in its own right, which scholars have long recognized as a distinct account supplied from a source differing from the chapter 1 account. Once again, food is at the forefront of the narrative. The vegetation mentioned in 2:5 is not so much a look back to the vegetation of 1:11–12 and 1:29–30 but rather looks ahead to the "thorns and thistles" of 3:18, which are a result of the sinful fall of humankind in the Garden of Eden. The landscape of the earth is about to change, and this is the direct result of human disobedience to God. Even the statement "the Lord God had not caused it to rain upon the earth" of 2:5 is probably anticipatory of 7:4, "I will send rain on the earth . . ." There apparently was no need for

3. Hafer, *Faith & Fitness*, 54.

rain before the flood because God's provision for water came from the earth itself, rather than the sky. This is seen in 2:6, "But a stream would rise from the earth, and water the whole face of the ground . . ." and in verse 10, "A river flows out of Eden to water the garden . . ." God had not only provided for the land to be self-producing as concerned food supply, but he also planned it so that even the water would come forth from the earth to supply the necessary liquid needed to sustain vegetation. I am reminded of a time I was standing in the produce section of a grocery store and leaning in to closely inspect the fruits and vegetables for purchase. As I leaned closer over the produce, I was surprised and nearly showered by a sudden sound and a spray of soft water that came on by a pre-set timer, implemented to provide consistent water nourishment to the array of fresh fruits and vegetables. It did not take much thinking to determine why there is not such a sprinkling system in the candy or processed food aisles. Water is life-giving. Fruits and vegetables are life-giving foods, and candies and processed foods are not. It is as if God in his earliest (pre-fall) design for the world had his own automatic sprinkling system to take care of his garden.

In fact, gardens in the mythology of the ancient world were viewed as places where the gods dwelt. In Genesis, the Garden of Eden most certainly represented a place where God would dwell and have fellowship with humankind (3:8). We have already seen that it was a place of abundant food (2:9, 16), thereby suggesting that the garden was a place where God was to be found, and in that place where God was to be found, there was food present. To a great extent, then, as will be seen throughout this study, the presence of food suggests the atmosphere of fellowship. To anticipate ahead to the book of Exodus, we see that Moses, Aaron, Aaron's sons, and seventy of the elders of Israel saw God in great glory, and that as they were beholding his majesty, they "ate and drank" (Exod 24:9–11). It is also of interest that when Israel was formed as a nation as recorded in Exodus and beyond, that part of their sanctuary worship would include what was known as the "Bread of Presence" (Exod 25:30), bread that was placed weekly before the Lord to be consumed only by the priests. It clearly teaches that one aspect of being in the presence of God and having fellowship with him involves eating. Adam and Eve enjoyed this sort of freedom in the garden, but some restrictions were applied (Gen 2:17). We may consider that today God has given us much freedom in what we can eat, but perhaps, and probably for different reasons than Adam and Eve, we should put some restrictions upon ourselves for what, when, why, and how we eat. Food, the very substance that gave our first ancestors life in God's garden, became the very object that led to their death.

THE ROLE OF FOOD AND EATING
IN TEMPTATION

The temptation account of Genesis 3 is certainly one of the most significant stories in the Bible, and it records for us how humanity realized mortality. Leaving aside debates about the historicity of the event, the story belongs to the human family as a portrait of how humankind lost the paradise of the Garden of Eden, and more importantly, proper relationship with God. It is noteworthy that not only are food and eating the starting points of the conversation between Eve and the serpent, but a form of the word "eat" also appears seventeen times in Genesis 3. Food, it has been demonstrated from the first two chapters of Genesis, was perhaps the greatest gift of God to humanity, humanity itself being God's crowning achievement of creation. Yet it is this very gift, food, that becomes the object of debate and discussion between the serpent and Eve, leading to the inaugural act of human disobedience. The first inkling of temptation is that "the tree was good for food" (Gen 3:6). This sort of appeal to the eyes is what continues to allure us toward that which we should not do, be it capital crimes or lesser acts of putting our hands in the proverbial cookie jar. The framework for the entire collapse of humanity in the all-important narrative of Genesis 3 is humans not resisting food. It is certainly a metaphor for the challenge of human life to not go and do what God has told us to not go and do. Perhaps there is no better way of explaining the human conundrum other than to put it in everyday, and usually two to five times a day, terms, that of eating food. Without it, we die. With it, but out of its proper context, we die.

The result of the temptation to eat and the eating of the forbidden fruit led to God's indictment against the serpent and humankind. The serpent is judged first for his part in initiating the event (Gen 3:14–15). Of the three indictments, the first against the serpent, the second against the woman, and the third against the man, only the serpent is actually cursed. The woman is not, and the man is not, but the ground is (Gen 3:17). The curse on the serpent is directly related to eating, "and dust you shall eat" (Gen 3:14), a motif followed throughout the Old Testament (Mic 7:17; Isa 65:25). The man will not have to eat dust, for he is not cursed as the serpent.[4] However, his ordeal will have to do with extracting food from the ground, which is the object under a curse. Like the serpent, the man's judgment will involve eating, "in toil you shall eat of it all the days of your life" (Gen 3:17). The gift of the ground is now cursed, and man will now toil to bring forth its produce, which was once easily supplied by God's provision. Man will have to work and labor hard to bring forth food from the ground. The toil that would go into every meal from this time forth would be a reminder of the terrible consequences of human failure in the garden. Man would have to seek out his livelihood for himself. His relationship to the ground is clearly seen in that his very name, Adam, is derived from the Hebrew word for ground (*adamah*). Not only was man created from the

---

4. Jesus taught a principle that the one who tempts receives greater condemnation than the one who is tempted (Luke 17:1–2).

ground, but it would also be his life-long task to cultivate it, and he would eventually return to it in this new concept of death (Gen 3:19). The ground, then, is his cradle, his home, and his grave. What was initially envisioned as a gift had become a curse. The grace of God in the soil and the productive power of the earth would now require man's lifelong attention and effort.

The events of Genesis 3 carry over to chapter 4, where the first sin in the garden had given way to the ultimate crime, the first murder. The occupations and labors of the two brothers, Cain and Abel, led to tension over agriculture and farming and work and reward. This foreshadowed the war and violence that was still to be seen in actual human history over issues of land, resources, work, and justice. Cain himself, the first murderer, was the first human to be cursed by God, a curse that was directly related to the difficulty of cultivating the ground (Gen 4:11–12).

Most human beings throughout time have lived in agrarian cultures. The present world of the United States and other Western nations are a radical departure from this, with most citizens having lost touch with nature and agriculture. America is especially a fast-food nation. Apart from the obvious loss of good nutrition and health, the fast-food mentality has taken the typical American far away from the realization of just how difficult it can be to bring forth food from the land. Processed, enriched foods are a mere shadow of what real, life-giving food brings forth from the earth. And because most of us never work the land and can get our food without more thought than what size burger or fries to purchase, we easily forget the biblical principles God put forth to our earliest ancestors regarding the difficulty of cultivating the land. We may have to work hard at our office or other types of jobs, but there is no identification with the land anymore, so we rarely make the connection that we work in order to survive. It might be a useful spiritual exercise and discipline to, besides the typical disciplines of prayer, worship, and Bible study, create room in our lives for quiet and solitude in places associated with land and agriculture. Vegetable gardening, for instance, can open great opportunities for spiritual reflection on the Adam and Eve and Cain and Abel stories, as discussed above. Being more grateful and prayerful for farmers, and even encouraging farming as a noble occupation, are other ways to reconnect to the early biblical truth of the hardness of life having a relationship to the difficulty of cultivating the land.

I recall once being amused by a young person in church who somewhat mockingly referred to the life of a monk as one who attends to his chores and his vegetable garden. I am now slightly ashamed by being amused at this, as I have come to realize that staying connected to the productivity of the land is a great devotional exercise that brings us back to our origins in the Garden of Eden account. And this comes from one whose thumb has been as non-green as can be imagined.

POINTS TO PONDER

1. Think before you eat!

2. Food is a gift from God!

3. Give thanks to God who "brings forth bread from the earth"!

4. God's hunger is different from our hunger. He hungers for justice, kindness, and humility!

5. Eating could be considered a time of fellowship with God!

6. God has given us freedom to eat, but we should not reject restrictions!

7. Be mindful of the labor that goes in to producing food!

8. Respect the land!

2

Food and Eating in Ancient Israel

U NDERSTANDING THE diet, customs, and manners of everyday life pertaining to food and eating for the ancient Israelites of the Old Testament gives the modern person some appreciation for the task of sustaining oneself in that culture. In this chapter we explore, first, the role of labor in everyday food preparation, and second, the role of food and eating in Israel's law code.

THE ROLE OF LABOR IN EVERYDAY LIFE FOOD PREPARATION

In the first chapter we examined the role of food and eating in creation and temptation, events of great magnitude. These events, as well as the rest of the events of Genesis 1 through 11, are typically considered in biblical scholarship as ancient Israel's pre-story, which firmly begins with the call of Abraham (Gen 12:1–3). The development of the Abraham story led to the formation of the nation of Israel in the days of Moses and beyond, which ultimately led to an established nation of Israel attempting to live in the land of promise in obedience to God. This, in essence, is the Old Testament. Respect and appreciation for this land was a vital part of the culture and theology of the Old Testament. Many songs and writings have been produced by the Jews over time that focus on the "*eretz Yisrael*," Hebrew for "the land of Israel." Even a casual acquaintance with current events informs one that this piece of real estate in the modern Middle East is the source of much conflict and turmoil between the present state of Israel and the Palestinian and Arab peoples. It was desired territory then, and it is desired territory today. Whereas in the present world the conflict is more about religion and politics, in the ancient world, the struggle was over the ease of food production and in general, survival. Farming and agriculture were generally much better in what today is known as Israel than it was in the surrounding desert areas.

For Old Testament Israel, the arrival in the land of promise in the days of Joshua provided a fresh approach to the harvesting of food. The previous wilderness wanderings proved God's faithfulness as he supplied the day-to-day rations needed for survival, both food and water (Exod 15–17; Num 20:8–11). This, however, would need to be seen in a different sort of way in their new homeland. God would not supernaturally drop the food in their laps or provide water from rocks,[1] but he did promise to send rain to bring forth the produce of the land (Deut 11:11–12). The harshness of harvesting would be less burdensome in this new land than in other parts of the world. This would be an experience far different from what they had seen while living as slaves in Egypt, a land without much natural rainfall, which caused the Egyptians hard labor, as they had to irrigate their crops with water from the Nile (Deut 11:10). On the contrary, the abundance of natural resources of the land of promise was captured in the summary phrase, "a land flowing with milk and honey" (Deut 11:9). The two terms "milk" and "honey" each connote something different. "Milk" is associated with the products of the herd—that is, all that sheep and goats provided. "Honey" is a by-product of

---

1. Despite the supernatural provision of the Lord throughout the forty or so years of wilderness wanderings, it is noteworthy that much of what angered the Lord during this time period was complaint about food and drink, witnessed on several occasions (Exod 15:24, 16:1–3, 17:1–3; Num 11:4–35, 20:1–13).

the farmer who cultivates fruit and olive trees, thereby attracting the honeybee with the blossoms of the trees.[2] In sum, "milk and honey" meant the land was good for both shepherds and farmers. The promise of "milk and honey," however, was threatened by Israel's disobedience upon arrival and settlement of the land of promise. The reap/sow retribution principle so typical of the book of Deuteronomy is apparent in the passage immediately following the "milk and honey" promise.

> Take care, or you will be seduced into turning away, serving other gods and worshiping them, for then the anger of the Lord will be kindled against you and he will shut up the heavens, so that there will be no rain and the land will yield no fruit; then you will perish quickly off the good land that the Lord is giving you (Deut 11:16–17).

Israel needed to think theologically about food and eating. Keeping the Lord's ways would ease the burden of readying a food supply because of God's provision of rain, which would indicate moving in a positive direction away from the cursing of the ground instituted in Genesis 3:17. The fact that Israel ended up ultimately cast away from the land into foreign exile proves their historic and continual disobedience. This was because they did indeed "serve other gods" (Deut 11:16), in particular, the god Baal, the storm god of the Canaanites who supposedly provided rain and an abundant harvest. The Israelites might have honored the Lord with their offerings and sacrifice, but many chose to save some for Baal, perhaps as an insurance policy, trying to be sure that they sought to honor all the gods. This was, of course, a drastic mistake, since Israel's God was God alone and he would not share the worship and affection of his people with the pagan deities. This was especially problematic in the north of Israel, considered to be the bread-basket of the land, where rainfall was more abundant, as well as depended upon. It is no wonder that

2. Frick, *A Journey Through the Hebrew Scriptures*, 41.

the northern kingdom of Israel went into exile long before the southern kingdom of Judah.

This temptation to trust in something other than the one true God for basic provision can manifest itself today in a variety of ways. As a starting point, failure to recognize that all of planet earth's natural resources are the gift and provision of God is idolatry on a par with ancient Baalism. All of human life is dependent upon God's hand of mercy. The further removed we are from nature and agriculture, and the more dependent we are upon technology and modernism, the greater the risk of ignoring faith in and thankfulness to God.

As a resident of Ohio, I have been fortunate to live near Amish communities most of my life. For all the oddities and peculiar differences that the Amish may have compared to mainstream American society, I cannot help but admire their simple and communal way of life. Whereas driving by hat-bearing, simply dressed horse and buggy riders in my youthful years might have evoked a negative, ignorant, and prejudiced response, I have found that in my adult years the experience has caused me to be prayerful, contemplative, and introspective. Perhaps I needed to reconsider the complexity of my life. Perhaps I lacked in manual labor, community responsibility, and agricultural/farming awareness. Maybe I was the strange one and not the Amish. Many of my contemporaries and those a generation or two before me will recall a well-known television commercial, advertised many years ago, that featured a Native American paddling a canoe through a polluted and what was then present-day river and landscape. His noble face displayed a tear streaming down his cheek in expression of the sadness that had gripped his heart as a result of a paradise lost due to consumerism and modernism. The commercial was poignant for its time. The loss of attachment and appreciation for the land continues all the more into our day, distancing us more and more from God the creator. Baal is worshiped once again.

Let us return to everyday life in ancient Israel. The climate of the land of promise had two distinct seasons annually, dry and wet, with 70 percent of the yearly rainfall occurring between the months of November and February.[3] There could potentially be many possible variations and transitions in climate, which could lend to farming being at times a tricky enterprise. The Deuteronomy notion of obedience bringing rain, as the farmer would have needed, extended late into the Old Testament period, so that even the theology of the book of Malachi spoke of God "opening the windows of heaven" (Mal 3:10), a beautiful metaphor, which in most English translations is rendered as "windows," but in the New International Version (NIV) is translated as "floodgates." This NIV translation is of interest because it captures the cosmic mindset of the ancients. That is, there was a belief in a three-tiered universe and that humanity, which occupied the second tier, was surrounded by water above and below. The opening up of the "floodgates" (aka "windows") would indicate God allowing a deluge onto the realm of humanity, not merely of rainwater, but also of the agricultural and financial bounty that would result. The Hebrew word for "window/floodgate" in Malachi 3:10 has a relationship to the Hebrew verb for "lurking or lying in wait to ambush."[4] The notion here then might be of the tremendous surprise that would come upon the Israelite worshiper and tither who honored the Lord and then was deluged with blessing. It is of course a pleasant surprise!

3. Ibid., 46.

4. In similar fashion, the well-known shepherd Psalm (Ps 23) states in verse 6, "Surely goodness and mercy shall follow me . . ." The Hebrew word for "follow" is not a passive lagging behind but rather indicates a pursuit that will overtake one. In other words, as in Malachi 3:10, the blessing, goodness, and mercy of God ambush the obedient one in a positive and surprising way.

Farming and agriculture as a way of life were really advancements from the earlier methods of gathering and hunting food. Rather than having to live nomadically, the Israelites could sow seed in one place, for that is what farming is. One might recall the story of Esau (we will have more to say about him in the next chapter), who, although a skilled hunter, nevertheless struggled in his effort to provide food for himself, having to give in to his more domestic brother (Gen 25:27–34). Nonetheless, the hardship of ancient farming had its own livelihood realities that could encounter a variety of obstacles, such as capricious water supplies, hot desert winds, locusts, erosion, and mud. Life was hard.

Self-sufficient farming was challenged in the early days of the Hebrew monarchy, as land was accumulated by the nobles at the expense of the original farmers. This was the prediction of the prophet Samuel (1 Sam 8:14). Isaiah would later give a similar indictment (Isa 5:8), and Nehemiah would eventually, late in Israel's Old Testament history, force a return of property to the original owners (Neh 5:11). The life of the typical Israelite was challenging, especially when there was disobedience. In the New Testament, the Apostle Paul spoke of his conversion as being encountered by Christ in the statement, "It hurts you to kick against the goads" (Acts 26:14). This is a farming metaphor that speaks of resisting to one's own detriment, like a beast of burden that goes in the opposite direction than it is being driven. Not only were hunting and farming difficult occupations, but so was virtually every other common trade, such as carpentry, fishing, pottery making, shepherding, metal-smithing, leatherworking, and stone masonry. Earning a living proved to be hard, as was promised in Genesis 3:17–19.

Whereas work was hard, food was simple. There were two basic meals of the day: breakfast and an evening meal.[5] Breakfast was informal, consisting of a cake of bread with olives, cheese,

---

5. This is verified by Jesus's own words in Luke 14:12, "When you give a luncheon or a dinner."

or dried fruit, often eaten by the men and boys as they went off to work for the day. The evening meal had similar contents, with perhaps vegetables, milk, and lentil stew scraped from a common pot, with bread being the most substantive staple. Fish and meat were rare and were considered luxury items. "Eating bread" was synonymous with having a meal (Gen 43:31–32; Luke 11:3).

I was privileged some years back to have a dear Christian friend from Malaysia who was studying theology with me at the University of Durham in England. He spoke English as a second or third language and would oftentimes invite me to eat with him via the expression, "Let us eat bread together." I learned to appreciate this simple, hospitable, and biblical way of wanting to share in Christian fellowship (although I did find some of his other idioms and expressions confusing and insulting, such as when he once said to me, "You have big nose." It was only later that I discovered he meant I had a cold!).

Apart from the basic diet just mentioned, salt would have been used for seasoning, and the only sweeteners would have been honey or a syrup made from boiled-down grape juice. This is a radical contrast to our sugar-crazed world today, which has yielded tragic and radical health results for present generations of Americans and others. The psalmist spoke of the ordinances of the Lord as being that which is sweetest of all, yes "sweeter also than honey, and drippings of the honeycomb" (Ps 19:9–10). Ralph Gower, in his book *The New Manners and Customs of Bible Times*, provides some insight into what life was like for Israelites:

> When a boy first went to school in New Testament times, he went down to the synagogue while it was still dark to listen to the story of how Moses received the law. Then he was taken to the teacher's house for breakfast, where he received cakes with letters of the law written on them. In school, the boy received a slate with passages from the Scriptures written on it. The slate was

> smeared with honey. He had to trace the letters through the honey with his pen, and it was natural to lick the nib of the pen as he proceeded. The idea was that he would realize that the purpose of his going to school was to absorb the Scriptures.[6]

The symbolism of the law of God being sweet like the honey is also obvious. Love of reading and studying Scripture should far exceed love of eating sweets, but unfortunately, this is typically not the case in our present culture. Manhood for the Hebrews was associated with the intellect and learning, especially Scripture, which is a far cry from our modern American masculinity, which takes its cues more from the classic Greco-Roman period of athletics and militarism.

As an additional thought, it should also be mentioned that the practice of hospitality was critical in the biblical world. Because getting food could be hard, the ancient traveler often depended upon the generosity of others for sustenance. Many people were acquainted with a nomadic way of life, something far removed from Western culture today. There was a realization that helping someone might have been a matter of life or death. God had condemned the Ammonites and Moabites for their lack of hospitality and food provision to the traveling Israelites (Deut 23:3–4). There was, in general, a great obligation in biblical culture to offer a meal to a guest (Luke 11:8), which was also an expression of friendship and peace (Gen 26:28–30), and because of the monotony and tedium of life, almost any excuse was given for a party and celebration. During the first few months of my study in England, my wife and I had opportunity to have dinner, or "tea," with folks from twenty-eight different nations around the world. On some occasions we were the hosts, and on others we were the guests. The shared meals were an expression of friendship and our common humanity, with long, pleasant, and enlightening conversations taking place. American culture

6. Gower, *The New Manners and Customs of Bible Times,* 86.

diet (Dan 1:5–16). Also, the Jewish food laws gave a good degree of protection from food poisoning when cooking temperatures were low. In sum, it appears that the food laws protected Israel from bad diet, dangerous vermin, and communicable diseases.[11]

Nonetheless, although health factors can explain why some food was branded as unclean, it does not account for all the items. It also makes little sense that Jesus himself would declare all foods clean in the first century of the Common Era if health and hygiene were the primary issues all along. The risk of illness and disease would not have changed much. Whatever the original reason for the food laws, and perhaps it is a combination of all four mentioned above, it is true that once upon a time in ancient Israel the food one ate was related to holiness. Although we can in no way press the ancient food laws as being applicable today, we should take seriously the spirituality that might be associated with our diet and eating as it was for the Israelites. Perhaps there is a hidden lesson in that there were unclean creatures from all three geographical areas: earth, sea, and sky. Land creatures, birds, and fish are all represented as having unclean elements so that there is no place one can go on the planet to escape the consequences of the fall of humanity in the Garden of Eden. The point might just be that there was no escaping the results of the Edenic curse. It makes sense, then, that when Jesus declared all animal food items clean, he was in essence declaring his eschatological and universal redemption. It might even be possible to imagine that the purpose of the ancient food laws was only to point the way forward to the coming of Jesus, so that, in effect, they were really nothing more than an object lesson to illustrate the Christian gospel.

11. Harris, "Leviticus," 569.

POINTS TO PONDER

1. God is the source of all our food!

2. Technology and modernism can cause us to lose our dependence upon God!

3. Consider living a simpler life!

4. Life was hard in the ancient world!

5. Food was simple in the ancient world!

6. Love study and learning more than eating!

7. Practice hospitality by sharing your food!

8. Eating once had a relationship to holiness!

3

Food and the Wisdom of Sages

IT WAS stated in the previous chapter that the Israelite law code included elements of diet and eating as having a part in how one related to God. In this chapter we shall explore how some of the later Israelite teachers and religious leaders, known as sages because of their wisdom, also included one's approach to food as playing a part in godliness. We shall examine first the topic of gluttony, and then we shall have a look at three narrative case studies from the Old Testament: Esau, Eglon, and Eli, each of whom has something to say about one's character being related to one's approach to food or poor physical condition.

GLUTTONY

The creation narrative of the opening chapters of Genesis that was discussed at the outset of this book established that food is a gift from God for humankind. The later sages of Israel understood this. The writer of Ecclesiastes, for instance, states, "Moreover, it is God's gift that all should eat and drink and take pleasure in all their toil" (Eccl 3:13). Or again, "Go, eat your bread with enjoyment, and drink your wine with a merry heart; for God has long ago approved what you do" (Eccl 9:7). Food is pleasurable and to be enjoyed, and although the sages knew this, they were aware that the law code warned of the dangers of a certain kind of eating that was associated with the loose morals of a young person who was a riotous eater and drinker (Deut 21:20) or what we might call today a partier. This is part of the portrayal of the well-known prodigal son of New Testament fame (Luke 15:11–32). Ironically, Jesus's opponents accused him of being somewhat of this sort of partier, a "glutton and drunkard" who was antithetical to the strict asceticism of John the Baptist (Matt 11:18–19) and those who kept the rigorous food laws. Although the charges against Jesus were distorted, it is obvious that those given to food and drink indulgence in Israelite culture were viewed in a very negative way.

The descriptive Hebrew term given to the self-indulgent over-eater of food in the Deuteronomy 21:20 passage is often translated in English versions of the Bible as glutton. This English word comes from the Latin *gluttire,* meaning "to gulp down or swallow." Gluttony eventually became known as one of the seven deadly sins of the medieval Christian Church, and the eternal consequences included being force-fed rats, toads, and snakes in hell, a punishment related to the crime. The act of gluttony became associated with the color orange. From the animal kingdom, its association was with—well, you can probably guess—the pig! It is easy to see where the popular vernacular insult to a fat person, "You're a pig," comes from. The reality of gluttony today is that the National Institute of Health has declared that one-third of all Americans, some sixty-three million, are overweight.[1] Three hundred and fifty thousand people in America die of obesity-related causes each year, and excess weight may soon pass cigarette smoking as the leading cause of preventable death.[2] America moves more and more in the direction of becoming both the Augustus Gloop (from *Willy Wonka and the Chocolate Factory)* and the Diamond Jim Brady of the world. It is said of Diamond Jim Brady, the railroad industrialist of the Gilded Age, that he:

1. Prose, *Gluttony,* 77.
2. Ibid., 69.

> Would begin his meal by sitting six inches from the table
> and would quit only when his stomach rubbed uncom-
> fortably against the edge. To that effect, he might con-
> sume, at a single dinner, dozens of oysters, some crabs,
> turtle soup, two ducks, several lobsters, a steak, rabbit,
> and just to keep healthy, various kinds of vegetables. For
> dessert he might eat an array of pastries and an entire
> box of chocolates.[3]

In essence, he became the personification of gluttony and a mirror, even if somewhat exaggerated, for us all to look into.

The sagacious writings in the book of Proverbs have a handful of comments about gluttony. For instance, 23:21 warns that "the drunkard and the glutton will come to poverty . . ." and 21:17 states that "whoever loves pleasure will suffer want; whoever loves wine and oil will not be rich." In fact, the person of great appetite is rhetorically admonished to "put a knife to the throat" (Prov 23:2), and in context it would appear that longing for food in an unhealthy way may go hand in hand with an unhealthy longing for wealth (Prov 23:1–8). For, so the sage says, "It is not good to eat much honey" (Prov 25:27), a statement that might have the dynamic equivalent today of "it is not good to eat much sweets." There is interesting poetic parallelism going on in 28:7, "Those who keep the law are wise children, but companions of gluttons shame their parents." The parallelism indicates that the young person has a choice of companionship: either hang out with the law of God and be wise or hang out with gluttons and become shameful. This verse teaches that one's desire should be for God and his words, not pleasure and partying. In the New Testament, the Apostle Paul taught moderation (Phil 4:5) and self-control (Gal 5:23), and he warned the Philippian church against those whose "god is the belly" (Phil 3:19) and the people of Crete about their gluttony (Titus 1:12–13).

3. Ibid., 84.

Besides the witness of the Bible, there has also been a witness from a variety of other sages throughout history, as well as philosophers and theologians, concerning the topic of gluttony. For instance, Aristotle urged moderation in food and drink consumption:

> Drink or food that is above or below a certain amount destroys the health, while that which is proportionate both produces and increases and preserves it. So too is it, then, in the case of temperance and courage and the other virtues. For the man who flies from and fears everything and does not stand his ground against anything becomes a coward, and the man who fears nothing at all but goes to meet every danger becomes rash; and similarly the man who indulges in every pleasure and abstains from none becomes self-indulgent, while the man who shuns every pleasure, as boors do, becomes in a way insensible; temperance and courage, then, are destroyed by excess and defect, and preserved by the mean.[4]

Another of the classical Greek writers and philosophers, Plutarch, compared the human body to a sailing ship that must not be overloaded with food and drink, lest it founder and sink.[5] Of course, the classical period of the great Greek thinkers and writers, such as Aristotle and Plutarch, gave way to the heyday of the Roman Empire, which apparently gave little heed to their counsel. Some of the Romans became known for their infamous vomitoriums, in which Roman hosts made provision for their guests to have unlimited capacity for culinary enjoyment by allowing them to eat to the point of puking, only to repeat the cycle so that they might not have to stop eating! Such Roman excess and decadence led to a certain amount of disgust on the part of Christians, as Christianity was developing in the early centuries beyond the earthly life of Jesus. Tertullian, the African

4. Aristotle, *The Nicomachean Ethics*, 29.

5. Prose, *Gluttony*, 25.

Christian theologian of the late second and early third centuries of the Common Era, expressed his horror at the mass belching that soured the air at the lavish Roman feasts and was appalled at the debt incurred by family dinner assemblies.

Tertullian begins for us a journey through some of the thinking of Christian theologians from antiquity to modernity on the topic of food, eating, and gluttony. We have thus far had in this book, and will continue to have, primarily a biblical investigation of food as it is to be understood in God's divine providence, for the Bible is a primary part of what theology, or at least Protestant theology, is. Thus when we call this work a "theological approach," we find that biblical analysis is completely consistent with what is intended. However, we should certainly all be aware that there is a tradition of commentary and theological thought that has developed over the centuries since the completion of the Bible, both the Old and New Testaments. This tradition consists of a whole host of Christian leaders, apologists, ministers, and formulators who could all be called "theologians." The following paragraphs, while not exhaustive, give us a synopsis of some of what has been said over these centuries by a few of the most influential Christian theologians, as well as some others, and helps us in considering what a "theological approach to eating, diet, and weight control" might look like.

Starting in the fourth century, three well-known theologians from Eastern Christianity expressed views about eating and gluttony. One of them, Basil (331–370 AD), also known as "the Great," and who was one of the three esteemed "Cappadocian Fathers," had a general concern for health as could be seen in his establishment of charities and hospitals. For him, there was a fairly direct link between gluttony and sexual lust. He stated:

> Through the sense of touch in tasting-which is always seducing toward gluttony by swallowing, the body, fattened up and titillated by the soft humors bubbling

> uncontrollably inside, is carried in a frenzy towards the
> touch of sexual intercourse.[6]

A second Eastern father, John Cassian (360–435 AD) shared this view. Being an ascetic, he became known for introducing Eastern monastic spirituality to the West. For him, like Basil, lust was at the end of the natural progression of vices set in motion by gluttony. He stressed the importance of bridling sensual temptation:

> Do not pity the body bitterly complaining of weakness,
> nor fatten it up with extravagant food . . . For if it re-
> covers, it will rise up against you and it will wage battle
> against you without truce . . . A body deprived of food is
> an obedient horse, and it will never throw off its rider.[7]

Perhaps Cassian was influenced by the prophet Jeremiah, who had likened the Judahites to "well-fed lusty stallions, each neighing for his neighbor's wife" (Jer 5:8). The horse of sexual lust is therefore bridled by first controlling the horse of desire for food and drink. A third contemporary Eastern father, John Chrysostom (347–407 AD), known for being a bishop and extraordinary preacher, came down hard on gluttony. He felt there was nothing worse or more shameful. He described the symptoms and signs of gluttony as "discharge, phlegm, mucus running from the nose, hiccups, vomiting, and violent belching . . . The increase in luxury is nothing but the increase in excrement."[8] I find Chrysostom's views to be similar to my own, even as I related in a story in the introduction of this book about over-fed passengers on trans-Atlantic flights. Recently, such a flight had an incident of backed-up toilets during the many hours of over-the-ocean travel in which raw human sewage flowed down the entire length of the airplane, filling the aisles of the passenger

6. Ibid., 14.

7. Shaw, *The Burden of the Flesh*, 75.

8. Ibid., 133.

compartments. Passengers were forced to fast out of necessity (and probably desire), and there would have been great appreciation from those on board toward anyone who had not used the facilities because of temperance before boarding the airplane.

There is one more theologian of the time period of Basil, Cassian, and Chrysostom who deserves more than passing mention. That, of course, is the famous North African, and arguably the greatest ever Christian theologian, Saint Augustine (354–430 AD). For Augustine, somewhat like and somewhat unlike Basil and Cassian, "The battle to subdue the urge to take delight in eating presented nowhere near the challenge of the corresponding struggle to remain chaste, and yet it posed the same problem: how to avoid the lures of enjoyment."[9] Augustine is known for some great classic literary works, foremost among them which might be his *Confessions.* Confession XXXI is specifically a short essay on the temptations and lusts of eating and drinking. He clearly discerned that food and drink were as "medicine of nourishment"[10] and that "health is the reason of eating and drinking."[11] It was not something he could cut off once and for all, as if there would be no further need of food and drink. He viewed concubinage this way—that is, although it was something he confessed to having a great struggle with, he could nonetheless divorce himself from any mistress without ever having to re-involve himself to sustain life, which is not the case with food and drink. He spoke of being in a "daily war"[12] in which he would have to "strive daily against longing for food and drink."[13] For Augustine there was a time when one might pass "from the uneasiness of want to the calmness of satiety,"[14] meaning that

9. Prose, *Gluttony*, 28.

10. Augustine, *Basic Writings,* 169.

11. Ibid., 169.

12. Ibid., 169.

13. Ibid., 171.

14. Ibid., 169.

food and drink are of course basic human needs that can move beyond necessity to indulgence, a sort of "Do we live to eat or eat to live?" kind of issue.

In the sixth century came Gregory the Great, a gifted church leader who would become pope from 590–604 AD. Gregory is credited with formulating the famous "seven deadly sins," of which gluttony is amongst them. According to him, gluttony could reveal itself in one of five ways: "too soon, too delicately, too expensively, too greedily, and too much."[15] By "too soon" Gregory meant that one eats before there is real need to eat; by "too delicate" he meant that one is too fussy or dainty about one's food choice and preparation; by "too expensive" he meant indulgence in costly foods; by "too greedily" he meant self-centered eating without regard for others; and by "too much" he meant, well, exceeding the obvious measure of refreshment or need.

For Gregory, gluttony was a mortal sin. His five-fold categories are useful for our own management of eating today. Eating "too soon" is common practically to all of us, seeing that we tend to eat because food is offered, available, or being served. Rarely do we eat in America because we are genuinely hungry! We tend to eat because we either want to or we think we are supposed to! Food is all too available! We have conditioned ourselves, like Pavlov's dog, to eat as a response to certain stimuli. Seldom do we really experience hunger pangs. "Too delicately" is basically a rebuke against picky eaters, and by this I do not mean the individual who is discretionary because he or she is attempting to eat healthy. Rather, I mean the one who, like a child, has not allowed his or her taste buds to mature or has not learned to appreciate the vast array of God's beautiful creative bounty of food. A well-balanced diet takes from every food group, but the picky or "delicate" eater, as Gregory calls it, has a narrow selection, usually at the expense of the healthier foods, like fruits and vegetables. Being a "meat and potatoes man" is nothing to be proud of but

15. Prose, *Gluttony*, 7.

rather is a point of shame. A general rule of thumb should be to put as much variety of color on one's plate as is possible. More shall be said in a moment on this issue of "delicacy."

The gluttony of eating "too expensively," Gregory's third category, may be carried out today by having extravagant tastes or throwing food away. The bill incurred for eating one meal at certain kinds of restaurants can quite possibly be greater than the monthly salary of people in third-world countries. Perhaps we need to take a hard look at our actual what I call "eating for entertainment" budget. And how might we eat "too greedily"? Next time you are in a public gathering where people are eating together, such as a family reunion or a church/company picnic, observe who gets in line first, how much and what selection of food one puts on one's plate, and how quickly one might go back for seconds. Who contributes food to corporate gatherings of eating? Who does not? For those who contribute, what do they contribute? Is it cheap? Is it healthy? When there are pre-set tables, observe where people sit, depending on the amount of salad or type of dessert that has already been provided. Watch how people might handle and exchange food, all for their own desires. Oftentimes the four areas of gluttony just discussed are overlooked and it is only the fifth and final category that comes to mind. This, of course, is eating "too much." Although most people are aware of this primary form of gluttony, few folks have actually trained themselves to stop eating before they are full. I think personally that I may indeed eat too much at nearly every meal that I have, and my suspicion is that most who will read this book do also!

Moving from Gregory in the early medieval period to persons in the late medieval period, two notable theologians come to mind, both of whom have different contributions to make regarding the topic of gluttony. They are Francis of Assisi (1182–1226 AD) and Thomas Aquinas (1225–1274 AD). Francis, the founder of the Franciscan order of Friars, is well known for his love of nature and simplicity, having forsaken a life of wealth to be inherited from his father and a family business in order to embrace a life of poverty and service. Tradition has passed down that when it came to enjoying food, Francis would destroy any hint of taste by sprinkling ashes on it. "Don't try this at home," would be my response, as the trajectory of this book contends that tasty food is a gift of God to be enjoyed and for which we can give God glory for his wonderful acts of creation. However, Francis's rigor demonstrates his concern for palatable pleasures weakening one's faith commitment, something that is a good reminder for us.

Aquinas, on the other hand, grew up as a slow, overweight child, which eventually earned him the nickname "the dumb ox." Although he is now known to us as being rather obese, he has also earned the distinction of actually being termed the "greatest medieval theologian."[16] He wrote the *Summa Theologiae*, commonly viewed as the supreme medieval theological system. In it he writes on moral virtue, of which moderation is a key topic for Thomas. His statements on moderation in food and drink are mostly concerned not with actual eating and drinking but with what he calls the "unregulated and unreasonable desire of it."[17] He is somewhat patient with the over-eater, perhaps a result of his own weight problem, in that he states that "eating too much thinking one needs it is not gluttony but inexperience . . . gluttony is knowingly eating too much pleasurable food for pleasure's sake."[18] For Thomas, as with Augustine, but unlike Gregory, gluttony is a lesser, venial sin, not a mortal sin. His softer stance may also have been an objection to the fact that in his day gluttony had made its way up near the top of the list of the seven deadly sins. However, Thomas nonetheless argued for gluttony's inclusion with the seven deadly sins, believing that it, like the

16. Bowden, *Who's Who in Theology*, 120.

17. Aquinas, *Summa Theologiae*, 428.

18. Ibid., 428.

other so-called deadly sins, led to other sins. These "daughters" of gluttony, as he called them, included "excessive and unseemly joy, loutishness, uncleanness, talkativeness, and an uncomprehending dullness of mind."[19] In certain respects, he appears to liken the results of over-eating to the state of intoxication, as if eating too much can put one in a drunk-like state.

I am reminded of when I worked as a traveling sales representative with my brother many years ago. Upon our trips to a particular Southern state, we would work all day without eating and then celebrate the end of the work day by dining at an all-you-can-eat buffet. The food, although rather generic, consisted of an array of numerous meats, starches, breads, fruits, vegetables, drinks, and desserts. We would consume what seemed like two to three days of food at a time, mostly in the name of "getting our money's worth," only to return to our hotel, plop on the beds, and at times, laugh uncontrollably in a state of near ecstasy. We were in a sense drunk, not on alcohol, but on food! The well-known verse from Ephesians 5:18 comes to mind: "Do not get drunk with wine, for that is debauchery; but be filled with the Spirit." What is perhaps key here is that the parallel antithesis to drunkenness is filling oneself, not with liquor, but with the Holy Spirit. In a similar sense one might get drunk on food, a debauchery in its own right, whereas one should seek the Spirit-filled life, which gives a different sort, indeed a godly sort, of ecstasy ("making melody to the Lord in your hearts," Eph 5:19). I shall think twice next time before entering an all-you-can-eat restaurant. Think before you eat!

In the century following Francis and Thomas, Dante, Chaucer, and Thomas a' Kempis, all commented on gluttony. Dante was an Italian poet who wrote the classic work *Inferno*, in which the glutton was assigned eternal punishment in the third circle of hell.[20] In Chaucer's written tales greed is the root of all

19. Prose, *Gluttony*, 14.
20. Ibid., 47.

evil, but greed itself is a byproduct of gluttony.[21] In his *Imitation of Christ*, Thomas a' Kempis stated "when the belly is full to bursting with food and drink, debauchery knocks at the door."[22]

As we move historically closer to modernity, the Spanish mystic who became known as St. John of the Cross (1542–1591) had a different take on gluttony. For him, there was a greater evil—spiritual gluttony. This had to do with those who in their pursuit of God had need of experiencing God with the natural senses:

> And thus they desire to feel and taste God as though He were comprehensible by them and accessible to them, not only in this, but likewise in other spiritual practices. All this is very great imperfection and completely opposed to the nature of God, since it is impurity in faith.[23]

St. John of the Cross wrote fervently about the "road of the cross,"[24] hence his descriptive name. He writes that "the soul that is given to sweetness naturally has its face set against all self-denial, which is devoid of sweetness."[25] For John, this "spiritual gluttony and inordinate appetite"[26] of having to experience God through the senses was weakness and something God would deny. John reminds us, then, of a basic Christian spiritual discipline and expectation—the need for self-denial. His hard stand on "spiritual gluttony" certainly carries over to physical gluttony. If the soul is not to be satisfied by "sweetness," then the body is not to be satisfied by "sweetness."

In the centuries since St. John of the Cross, Christians like David Brainerd (1718–1747) and Ignatius Brianchaninov (nine-

---

21. Ibid., 15.
22. Pleij, *Dreaming of Cockaigne*, 372.
23. St. John, *Dark Night of the Soul*, 56.
24. Ibid., 57.
25. Ibid., 57.
26. Ibid., 57.

teenth century) have demonstrated in word and deed the need for moderation in food and drink. Brianchaninov, an Eastern Orthodox leader, is known for his teaching that temperance of the stomach leads to virtues; and Brainerd, who carried out missionary work to Native Americans, is known for his strenuous practice of discipline. Brainerd's spiritual diary, edited by Jonathan Edwards for publication after his premature death, revealed a rigorous devotion in Brainerd's missionary task that involved disciplining his stomach with a minimal amount of daily food. Why, even Hannibal was known for training his stomach in moderation for his military task. American servicemen fighting the twentieth-century wars in the Pacific and Southeast Asia became aware of how the enemy soldiers were capable of operating for days on just one bowl of rice.

In the twentieth century, C. S. Lewis, the English novelist and apologist, wrote many popular books on Christianity and is more of a household name today than perhaps any other Christian thinker and writer. In one of his well-known works, *The Screwtape Letters*, Lewis addressed the topic of gluttony. The book itself is a creative and imaginary correspondence between devils who happen to be discussing various strategies for ensnaring the human populace. This diabolic attempt to keep people from properly serving God is a family affair, for one devil is the uncle (Screwtape) of the other (Wormwood). Screwtape is the experienced devil who, via a series of letters, instructs the younger Wormwood. Letter XVII is specifically devoted to the issue of gluttony. Here, Screwtape teaches about a spiritually blinded old woman who, thinking she is avoiding waste, practices the "gluttony of delicacy, not gluttony of excess."[27] She is in effect "fussy" when it comes to food. Lewis states, "She never recognizes as gluttony her determination to get what she wants, however troublesome it may be to others."[28] He gives the example of the

27. Lewis, *The Screwtape Letters*, 86.
28. Ibid., 87.

woman causing an overworked waitress in a crowded restaurant more stress by making her take her food back to be re-cooked. In fact, a recent quiz on gluttony conducted over the Internet posed the question, "How frequently do you send food back in a restaurant?" This is the gluttony of delicacy that Gregory the Great once wrote of and which Lewis has revived.

I recall a college roommate who constantly sniffed any food he was offered by others. The obnoxious habit eventually became a point of offense, as those who were willing to share were watching their food being scrutinized with nostrils delicately sniffing an inch away. In effect, any such dainty obsession with food is an act of gluttony, as Gregory and C.S. Lewis have indicated. Many of the recent American fad diets promote this sort of obsession, as they have people spending hours and hours per week counting calories, filling in charts, planning menus, and going through extra trouble in ordering and preparing food. This is not to say that an initial indoctrination and education on the topics of nutrition, diet, and the like would not be a worthy investment, but beyond a season of learning and training, one should get on with the business of living without devoting so much time and energy to what one will eat, especially when much of the world goes hungry and many of these folks are already overweight. There is a certain amount of discomfort to be expected in life, but instead of becoming strong by suffering life's minor inconveniences, the glutton of delicacy insists on being pampered at the expense of others. Being too fussy about one's food is an act of gluttony on a par with one who eats anything, anytime, anywhere.

Gluttony, then, is multi-dimensional and is disdained by many voices for many reasons over a lengthy period of time. It may or may not be a deadly sin, but according to the Old Testament, as well as to other writers and thinkers, it is bad behavior.

OLD TESTAMENT CASE STUDIES:
ESAU, EGLON, AND ELI

We began our study in this chapter by examining what Old Testament sages had to say on the topic of food and gluttony and then expanded our investigation to explore the views of philosophers and theologians as well. We now return to the Old Testament, and in particular, three case studies of persons who have issues with food and gluttony. These three persons, Esau, Eglon, and Eli, are portrayed in the narrative sections in which they are found in such a way so as to associate their relationship to food and fatness with their very character. Needless to say, it is all negative. The writers of these stories are sages in their own right, speaking volumes to us about these individuals by describing their less than desirable physical characteristics. They do so not with the tools of Hebrew poetry and parallelism but rather in descriptive narrative form.

The first case study thus portrayed is Esau. Esau is not fat or physically undesirable. In fact, he is quite the opposite, a "man's man," if you will, loved by his father Isaac. He is masculine, described as "hairy" (Gen 25:25; 27:11), and a "skillful hunter, a man of the field" (Gen 25:27). His story is set within the context of the early biblical patriarchal narrative, which is during the times of the Hebrew fathers: Abraham, Isaac, and Jacob. Abraham, originally known as Abram, received a promise from God that he would be the father of a great nation that would occupy a special land of promise. His story, as well as those of his son Isaac and grandson Jacob, is filled with ups and downs and successes and failures. Esau is the twin brother of Jacob, and their sibling rivalry began in the womb (Gen 25:22) and extended well into adulthood (Gen 32:6). They eventually become two nations, Israel (Jacob) and Edom (Esau), with a continued history of hostility.

Thinking historically, biblical commentator Claus Westermann has viewed the tension between Jacob and Esau as a sort of "history of civilization."[29] For him, the story is an oral tradition that developed in antiquity to capture the transition from hunting and gathering to shepherding and farming in the human drama. Jacob represents the new, emerging way of life; Esau represents that which is becoming outdated. In a similar vein, Hermann Gunkel understands the story to be depicting the superiority of the shepherd and farmer over the hunter and gatherer in that whereas the hunter slaughters animals, the farmer raises animals.[30] One brings animals to extinction for immediate needs, and the other thinks about having animals for tomorrow's food. In the story of the twin brothers, Jacob has foresight, since he is already planning beyond the death of his father. Esau is a man of the moment. He is rash and undisciplined. The theories of Gunkel and Westermann are certainly speculation, but they nonetheless offer interesting insight as to how the biblical narrative may have developed. It seems quite certain, however, that an important moral in the story of Jacob and Esau is that life presents contests and that in this particular contest, the prudent man (Jacob) defeats the gluttonous man (Esau). This then will be our concern for the purposes of this book as we investigate some of the details of the story.

To begin with, it is of interest that the contest between the brothers of trying to win their father's favor is set in motion by their father desiring a certain kind of food (Gen 25:28; 27:9, 14). At the root of the struggle, then, is the desire to eat something, similar to the foundational Adam and Eve story. Esau comes home from an unsuccessful day of hunting wanting to eat. His weakened physical condition from lack of nourishment is emphasized. The Bible says, "He was famished" (Gen 25:29), and it comes from his own lips, "I am famished" (Gen 25:30).

29. Westermann, *Genesis 12–36*, 417.

30. Gunkel, *Genesis*, 291.

Everything becomes embellished for Esau. "I am about to die; of what use is a birthright to me?" (Gen 25:32). This not really near-death experience is somewhat emulated in later Old Testament portrayals through the pity parties, to a lesser extent, of Elijah (1 Kgs 19:4, 10) and to a greater extent, of Jonah (Jonah 4:3, 8, 9). Esau exaggerates and cannot see beyond the moment. His brother Jacob has prepared a meal, and Esau wants it, regardless of the cost or consequences. Like a fool, he is ready to rush in. His lust and gluttony set an example for all to be cautious and temperate in seeking to satisfy the flesh. History is replete with story after story of sexual escapades that were carried out without proper forethought, leading to sexually transmitted diseases, divorce, unwanted pregnancies, and countless broken homes and broken hearts. Esau is the spiritual father of all those who act so irrationally and spontaneously. The desire to fill his belly on one occasion will forever change his future in a negative sense.

Esau doesn't even seem to know or care what the food is, as he says, "Let me eat some of that red stuff" (Gen 25:30). His behavior throughout the episode is rash, rough, and coarse. The Hebrew word for "eat" here is really "swallow," the basic definition of gluttony in the Latin, as was stated earlier. This is the only time this Hebrew word is used in the entire Old Testament. This distinctive act of gluttonous swallowing belongs to Esau alone. His request is rather desperate in his desire to gulp the "stuff" down. The scene would almost be humorous if it wasn't so catastrophic. Desperate eating, however, is familiar to many households in America today and not due to genuine hunger but rather due to inordinate affection for food. There can be a little, or a lot, of Esau in all of us—eating without thinking! Being the lover of game that Esau was, it is entirely possible that he thought what Jacob had prepared was meat, hence the reason he called the "stuff" red (Gen 25:30). Gerhard von Rad comments that Esau may have thought the meal was "blood soup,"[31] meat, that is, thereby be-

31. Von Rad, *Genesis*, 261.

ing further without his senses, not realizing that it was probably the common meal of "bread and lentil stew" (Gen 25:34). Like someone parched in the desert who sees an oasis mirage, so Esau is seeing things. Basically, the whole comic scene demonstrates that Esau acts like an all-around glutton. His foolish action is captured by five verbs strung closely together: he "ate," "drank," "rose," "went," and "despised" (Gen 25:34). He devours everything and leaves as if nothing happened. He is well-fed for now, so he is unconcerned with the future, even though he has sold it away. So it is with the gluttonous and over-indulgent.

The writer of the New Testament book of Hebrews has his own take on this story. For him, Esau's actions are "immoral and godless" (Heb 12:16), strong terms that emphasize how earthly minded Esau was. "Godless" is an especially harsh term, applied to Esau almost certainly because he was only concerned with the here and now. Godly folks have greater considerations beyond any given moment. Those who would control their eating, diet, and weight must be this sort of a person, not "like Esau . . . who sold his birthright for a single meal" (Heb 12:16). Numerous decisions are made by each of us every day in regard to what, when, and how much we will eat. We should not continue to sell out our future for meals of the moment again and again. It is an amazing statement worth pondering: "Who sold his birthright for a single meal," "Who sold his birthright for a single meal," "Who sold his birthright for a single meal." I have paid a steep price for a single meal at a few extravagant restaurants in my life but never an entire inheritance, especially the size of what Esau had coming to him, seeing that there was some wealth in the family. One might say that Esau paid thousands upon thousands of dollars, maybe more, for what would be a common home-cooked meal. I just purchased a sandwich today for two or three dollars more than it seems I should have paid for it, and I feel ripped-off. It wasn't even that good. Esau's purchase might be the worst deal of the centuries! Let us learn to be prudent and not indulgent. Once Esau realized his mistake, unfortunately, there was no going back (Heb 12:17).

On a different but related topic, I have made jogging a lifelong habit. And now that I am in mid-life I find that even though running is more challenging, the habit is so ingrained that it would be harder for me to not run than to run. Many times I see folks who are also in mid-life or beyond who have clearly neglected their weight and exercise. I observe them taking power walks in a desperate attempt to make up for all the lost time wasted on poor health habits and over-eating. I commend their efforts, but in a sense, they are like Esau, earnestly trying to change the consequences of bad decisions made in the past. Determine to not let this happen to you. Unlike Esau, start making good decisions today, particularly in regard to food, eating, diet, and weight control!

A lesser-known Old Testament character who needs mention in this discussion of gluttony is Eglon, the Moabite king of the early Israelite Judges period. Eglon bullied the Israelites by occupying a portion of their good land (Judg 3:13) and exacting tribute from them (Judg 3:15). It is possible that the tribute was a large of amount of food, seeing that the Israelites sent an entourage in order to please the king (Judg 3:18). Most notable, however, is that Eglon is described as a "very fat man" (Judg 3:17), a parenthetical descriptor that is important for the development of the story. The later prophets Jeremiah and Ezekiel admonished against a certain kind of fatness that was abundant in food and careless ease and that had no regard for the afflicted and marginalized of the world (Jer 5:28; Ezek 16:49). In today's vernacular we might call them "fat cats," those who are smug and have power and control but little regard for others. Eglon was a fat cat, physically and metaphorically, and is indeed the villain of the story.

In contrast to Eglon is the Israelite hero from the tribe of Benjamin, Ehud, who becomes the deliverer in the story. The

narrator, who has applied an obvious negative physical characteristic to Eglon, also applies a physical characteristic to Ehud.
Ehud is "left-handed" (Judg 3:15), a characteristic of Benjamites
but not a characteristic of most other people of the time. In other
words, Ehud had a rather unique skill. Not only could he wield a
sword as a southpaw, but he also had the skill and stealth to make
and hide on his person a custom-built sword with which he
could surprise the oppressive king, Eglon. Throughout the story
this Eglon appears fat, slow, and dull in the senses, whereas Ehud
is crafty, cunning, and slick. He is able to conceal his weapon
(Judg 3:16), and he is able to secure a private meeting with the
king (Judg 3:19–20), thereby giving him opportunity to strike a
death blow and deliver his people from this foreign glutton. After
killing the king, he escapes unnoticed, almost in the fashion of a
superhero in a modern movie. The contrast between Ehud and
Eglon is axiomatic. It is a contest for survival and quality of life,
similar to what we have just seen in the Jacob/Esau incident.
Eglon's fatness, according to the story teller, is a blunt and to the
point catch-all of his character and his fate. He will no doubt
eventually lose in the story, and when he does, it is to the sleek,
witty, and fit Ehud.

The account of the actual murder is described with great
attention to detail (Judg 3:20–25). The king is off guard, sitting alone and trying to keep cool. He only arises when Ehud
states he has a message from God for him, at which point the
fat king arises from his comfort only to take a mortal wound
to the part of his anatomy that is most exposed: his belly. His
huge size may have even prevented him from being able to see
Ehud's left-handed move. The narrator, however, is not content to
let us know that the king was stabbed and left for dead. Instead,
he provides gruesome details, ". . . the hilt also went in after the
blade, and the fat closed over the blade, for he did not draw the
sword out of his belly; and the dirt came out" (v. 22). The proper
translation of the word "dirt" here is speculative, as the Hebrew

term is found only here in the entire Old Testament. "Anus" may be a better way to understand it, so that in effect Eglon is disemboweled in one way or another.

The writer has chosen to give attention in the story to Eglon's fatness and now to his humiliating and horrible death. It is as if his death is related to his life. He lived enlarging his belly, and he died having his belly and related organs violently removed. But the narrator does not stop there. He goes on in verse 24 to describe how the king's servants became nervous over the king's delay, thinking that he was "relieving himself in the cool chamber." The literal Hebrew reads that he was "covering his feet," a phrase that can be used as a euphemism for one emptying the bowel or bladder (1 Sam 24:3). To put it another way, they may have thought that their king was on the "other throne"—what we call today "using the bathroom." In essence, Eglon is a comic figure like Esau. The giveaway in the text is that this king was a "very fat man" (Judg 3:17). Stories in the Bible such as this might make us uncomfortable, especially if we should find ourselves fitting the physical description of Eglon. Nonetheless, such stories should not be easily dismissed, as they provide details to make moral and ethical points. In this case, and as hard as the lesson might be, to be fat like Eglon is to be associated with Eglon; to be stealthy like Ehud is to be heroic.

Our third and final Old Testament narrative case study on food and gluttony has to do with the Israelite high priest Eli, who lived during the time of Samuel's youth. Eli, like Eglon, is characterized as "fat" (1 Sam 2:29), as well as "old and heavy" (1 Sam 4:18). However, unlike Eglon, he is an Israelite leader, not a foreign dictator. One might expect the heathen ruler to be a glutton, but an Israelite high priest who attended to the ark of God most certainly should not be. His physical lethargy is no doubt metaphorical for the spiritual lethargy that was plaguing the entire nation (1 Sam 3:1–3). Eli is a rather tragic figure during this stage of Israel's history. The nation needed help during the turbulent and troubled times that Eli was in leadership, and young Samuel was to be the solution.

The story of Samuel and Eli begins with an Israelite woman named Hannah and her husband Elkanah. Hannah was barren and was often provoked by her husband's other wife because she herself had provided numerous children to her husband (1 Sam 1:1–7). Hannah's response was to weep and fast (1 Sam 1:7–8). Her rigorous ascetic action will serve as a contrast to the lazy lethargy of Eli. Hannah is a heroine in this story, even though she will soon be overshadowed by the son (Samuel) that the Lord provides for her. She finally eats, after encouragement from her husband (1 Sam 1:9), and then appears at the temple of the Lord where Eli the priest is. She quietly and privately, yet earnestly and with great distress, prays a heartfelt prayer, asking for a son whom she is willing to dedicate to the service of the Lord (1 Sam 1:10–13).

She shows her personal commitment to a disciplined lifestyle in that she will give her son, should she be granted one, to priestly service and will keep strict physical vows, such as never having a razor come on his head. And what does she get in return for her vow of devotion? An accusation by the priest Eli of being drunk (1 Sam 1:14)! Eli is unable to recognize that the woman is earnestly seeking God. Was he not a priest? Should he not know what it was to seek God with passion? He is quick to judge and condemn the distressed woman but cannot see his own gluttony and the abusive behavior of his sons (1 Sam 3:13), who also were priests, and to whom he offers a mild and meaningless rebuke (1 Sam 2:22–25). Hannah respectfully defends herself, proclaiming that it is her soul that she has poured out, not strong drink (1 Sam 1:15). Eli finally comes around, and after providing encouragement and support to Hannah, she eats and goes away contented that the Lord will grant her petition (1 Sam 1:12–18), which of course he does. It is one of those encounters where laity has greater spirituality and discernment than clergy; and Hannah's greater spirituality in the first chapter of the book of 1 Samuel has been reinforced by her rigorous approach to food. Her beautiful prayer of thanksgiving for God providing her a son incorporates a symbolic food reference:

> Those who were full have hired themselves out for bread, but those who were hungry are fat with spoil. The barren has borne seven, but she who has many children is forlorn (1 Sam 2:5).

As Jacob is superior to Esau and Ehud is superior to Eglon, now Hannah is superior to Eli. And what do Esau, Eglon, and Eli have in common, besides that their names all begin with the letter E? They are all characterized as gluttonous in one way or another.

There are other participants in this story to reflect upon, as we consider the topic of food and gluttony. Eli's sons, for instance, previously mentioned briefly, display behavior that is indicative of Eli's own spiritual (and physical) lackadaisicalness (1 Sam 2:12–17). They commit a "very great sin" by "treating the offering of the Lord with contempt" (1 Sam 2:17). They steal the meat of the people's sacrifice "by force" (1 Sam 2:16) and demand raw, not boiled, meat for roasting (1 Sam 2:15). Their rude, riotous, and intrusive acts of bullying and thievery are topped off with gluttony that is reminiscent of the dainty and finicky food obsession that Gregory the Great and C.S. Lewis warned of. They can't have boiled meat, only raw meat for roasting. We saw earlier that both Basil and John Cassian believed that there was a link between gluttony and sexual lust. There certainly is such a link with Eli's sons, for not only were they indulging in the meat offered for sacrifice, but they were also fornicating with women who served at the doorway of the tent of meeting (1 Sam 2:22)!

There is another character, a rather shadowy figure, who enters into the narrative. He is simply known as "a man of God" (1 Sam 2:27). This man of God appears out of nowhere to rebuke the household of Eli and prophesy judgment upon it (1

Sam 2:27–36). Part of the chastisement against Eli and his sons is for "fattening" themselves with the people's offerings (1 Sam 2:29). The terminology that is used here in verse 29, literally "you *kicked* at my sacrifice," is found in the Old Testament only here and in Deuteronomy 32:15[32] where Israel is scorned for becoming fat, bloated, and gorged, only to *kick* at their God. The meaning of "kick" is to trample down and despise. The picture is as that of one who bites the hand that feeds it, perhaps like a child who grows big and fat and then turns on his or her parents by physically using his or her excess weight to overpower them. Ironically, the ending point of the man of God's rebuke is a reference to the household of Eli begging bread (1 Sam 2:36).

Basically, the entire narrative of the Eli/Samuel story is given flavor by the pathetic portrayal of Eli as a fat, old priest with dimming eyesight (1 Sam 4:15), all of which serve as emblems of the spiritually weakened state of the entire nation during this stage of Israel's history (1 Sam 3:1–3). Eli's gluttony is just one part of the problem, but nonetheless, it is part of the problem. The moral weakness of both him and his sons, especially because of their role as leading priests, demands divine intervention. Thankfully, Samuel will mature into what is needed for the spiritual vitality of the nation. As a boy he can be seen postured near the ark of God (1 Sam 3:3), whereas Eli is almost always depicted as being in a seated position (1 Sam 1:9; 4:13). And this is how we see him in his final moments, his death even being related to his weight condition:

> When he mentioned the ark of God, Eli fell over backward from his seat by the side of the gate; and his neck was broken and he died, for he was an old man, and heavy . . . (1 Sam 4:18).

32. This well-known "Song of Moses" speaks of Israel having been well nourished by God but now having become over-indulged.

I am reminded of an episode in a popular television comedy that portrayed the young husband and wife being challenged by the rigorous physical activity of another married couple in their age group. This other couple had kept a photo album of memories that included skiing, hiking, traveling, biking, and a whole host of other physical activities, while the primary couple did not possess one single photograph of themselves in a non-seated position. In similar fashion, the description of Eli as fat and lazy in the book of 1 Samuel is not very flattering. Likewise, Eglon's obesity described in Judges and Esau's foolish and gluttonous action in Genesis are written to provide us with models of how not to behave. And as we have seen in this chapter, gluttony and its associated sins has been on the radar screen for not only ancient Israelite sages and narrators to address, but also for classical philosophers, medieval theologians, and contemporary thinkers.

POINTS TO PONDER

1. Hunger for the word of God, not food!

2. A body deprived of food is an obedient horse!

3. Avoid eating . . .

   - "too soon"!
   - "too delicately"!
   - "too expensively"!
   - "too greedily"!
   - "too much"!

4. Moderation is a moral virtue!

5. Self-denial is a spiritual discipline!

6. Think before you eat!

7. Today's action leads to tomorrow's consequence!

4

Food and Eating in the Life
and Teaching of Jesus

Iɴ ᴛʜɪs chapter we turn our attention to Jesus, the greatest of
all sages, who is known for wisdom exceeding that of Solomon
(Matt 12:42). There are numerous teachings and actions involving
food in the life and ministry of Christ. For instance, in Matthew's
gospel alone there are lessons involving food on: the harvest
(9:37–38), wisdom (11:18–19), the Sabbath (12:1–7), character
(12:33–37), the word and kingdom of God via parables (ch. 13),
defilement (15:11), need and the miraculous (15:32–39), faith
and faithfulness (ch. 21), calling and being chosen (22:1–14), and
eating and drinking as an act of self-indulgence while disregard-
ing God (24:38–39). Of course, Mark and Luke, like Matthew,
are known as synoptic gospels, meaning "common view" because
of their use of similar stories and teachings, including many of
these same pericopes. The story of the rich man and Lazarus is
an example of a teaching of Jesus that is exclusive to Luke alone,
and in it, we see the parody of rich and poor, one eating in luxury
and the other a beggar, only to witness a complete reversal of
roles in the afterlife (Luke 16:19–31).

However, there are two very crucial events in the life of
Jesus described in the synoptic gospels that appear early in each
of the narratives that we will explore for our purposes of a theological approach to food. They are first, the temptation of Jesus
in the wilderness, which in one very important aspect involves
food; and second, the Sermon on the Mount, which incorporates

some useful lessons about how we think about food. The fourth gospel, the gospel of John, is unique. In it we shall see how water and bread are used by Jesus as metaphors for spiritual life and vitality. Jesus's invitation near the end of the gospel to "come and dine" (John 21:12 KJV) is a figure of speech far beyond sharing a morning meal. And really, the basic thesis of this book is that we need to shift our thinking from self-indulgent dining in the flesh to a more self-sacrificial and contemplative dining in the spirit.

THE SYNOPTIC GOSPELS

Matthew, Mark, and Luke each describe the temptation of Jesus in the wilderness early in their gospels following his baptism. For Matthew in particular, the heavenly statement at his baptism, "This is my Son, the Beloved, with whom I am well pleased" (Matt 3:17), prepares the reader for a primary tenet of Matthew's theology, which is that Jesus is indeed the Son of God. Jesus's own people will reject him because of this claim (Matt 27:40, 43), but pagans will recognize this truth (Matt 27:54). Jesus's final claim to have "all authority" is a proclamation of his divine sonship (Matt 28:18–20). This "obedient son" motif would have resonated well with Jews, who were certainly aware of Old Testament Israel's disobedience as the divine son (Deut 8:5; Hos 11:1–2). What Israel failed to do, specifically during the forty years of wandering in the wilderness, Jesus successfully did during his forty days of wilderness temptations. The children of Israel died in the wilderness with bread (Heb 3); Jesus lived faithfully in the wilderness without bread.

There are certainly similarities between not only Jesus and the Israelites but also between Jesus and Moses, who himself lived and fasted in the wilderness for forty days (Exod 34:28). All three of these wilderness situations, each of which revolve around the number forty, were similar time periods of testing and preparation, each for their respective tasks. Israel was to prepare herself for the land of promise, something she failed to do in a miserable fashion. Moses was preparing for his task of mediating God's law to the people, something he did with much faithfulness, until a moment prior to entering the promised land (Num 20:12). But Jesus was completely faithful! He defeated the devil in the wilderness, and for that matter, beyond the wilderness. And although it is appropriate to make connections concerning Jesus with both Moses and the Israelites, perhaps the most significant association is between Jesus and Adam. What Adam failed to do in the garden of temptation, Jesus faithfully accomplished in the wilderness of temptation. Whereas Adam, the first man, indulged in food he was commanded to abstain from, Jesus was unwilling to turn stones into bread to satisfy his hunger.

Interestingly enough, Luke appears to make the association between the first Adam in the garden and Jesus, the second Adam, in the wilderness.[1] Unlike Matthew and Mark, who tie Jesus's baptism directly to the wilderness temptation, Luke inserts the genealogy of Jesus between the two events. In so doing, the Lukan text suggests a contrast between Jesus and Adam, whose name is mentioned at the very end of chapter 3 (Luke 3:38), just prior to the temptation in the wilderness story (Luke 4). Luke therefore provides the reader with "a contrast between Adam, who though tested in the bliss of Eden yet fell, and Jesus, who was tested in the hardships of the wilderness yet triumphed."[2]

Mark is characteristically abbreviated in his description of the temptation in the wilderness, devoting only two verses to the subject (Mark 1:12–13). He does not describe the temptation as something that has a conclusion but may indeed have purposely left the story without ending so as to suggest that temptation will be a continuous, on-going struggle. One biblical commentator explains it this way:

1. The Apostle Paul was definitive in making this comparison (Rom 5:12–21; 1 Cor 15:21–22).

2. Carson, "Matthew," 111.

No specific temptations are described and no victory
over Satan is recorded. By this Mark wants to emphasize
that Jesus' entire ministry was one of continuous encounter with the Devil and not limited to a few temptations
in the desert during a period of forty days. Indeed, in his
Gospel he vividly describes this continuing conflict.[3]

Perhaps we need to consider that whatever struggles ex-
ist for us with food and eating are in like manner a continuous
battle, one that can be a day-to-day conflict that can only be
overcome through proper theological thinking and approach.
Fad diets often fail because they are momentary. One has success
only while on the diet. Stories of folks who lose a considerable
amount of weight in a short time, only to gain it all back again,
are numerous. Good theological thinking, however, will enable
one to recognize that victory over gluttony and food indulgence
is accomplished by making numerous good decisions on a daily
basis. Think before you eat! Adam (and Eve) is the model of failure—grab and partake! Jesus is the model of victory—think in
spiritual terms and overcome!

And just how does Jesus think and act theologically to
overcome the devil's temptations in the wilderness? It has always
been a curiosity to me that Matthew claims that hunger did
not come to Jesus until "afterwards" (Matt 4:2). That is, he was
not hungry until after forty days and forty nights of fasting. He
did this as a human being led by the Spirit of God, in a similar
fashion to any of us who are trying to accomplish something by
the power of God. Even as I write these words my stomach is
reminding me that I have gone many, many hours without food;
and yet I know that I really am not as much in need of food as
I would like to think I am. In fact, I am experiencing a so-called
hunger pang that comes and goes, and when it goes, the desire to
eat does not come again for quite some time. Our bodies can endure more than we know. However, we rarely give them a chance

3. Wessel, "Mark," 623.

to be tested, as food is all too available and we seldom pass up an opportunity to eat. Hunger can teach us dependence upon God and obedience, as seen in the wilderness events of Moses, the Israelites, and Jesus. As they were being prepared for their respective tasks, so perhaps we too need times of food denial so that we may prepare for our respective tasks. Because hunger is rarely forced upon the majority of us, we may have to force hunger upon ourselves.[4]

As previously mentioned, the gospel according to Matthew establishes the trajectory of Jesus as the obedient Son of God. It is clear that the tempter knows this in that twice he challenges Jesus with the statement "if you are the Son of God" (Matt 4:3, 6) do such and such. The first of these temptations is of course to turn stones into bread. The allurement here is for Jesus to use his God powers to satisfy his hunger and not with an elaborate feast but with some simple loaves. Temptation oftentimes starts small. In Genesis, it was a simple piece of forbidden fruit (Gen 3), which by the next chapter (Gen 4) had snowballed into the sin of murder, a full-blown attack on the very sacred image of God. Allurement to food indulgence can be the same way. One donut becomes a half-dozen, a piece of brownie becomes the entire pan, and a single cookie becomes an entire package. How, then, does one overcome this temptation? By thinking and acting like Jesus. Curiously, his entire ministry could be characterized as giving his own body to be broken and eaten like bread for others (Matt 26:26). He did not view his life as a desire to *eat* food but rather to *be* food. He came to give his life for others. This in essence is the Christian gospel and the mandate for all Christians—to not serve ourselves, but rather to serve others.

I am reminded of my Bible college experience where a great missionary who had traveled to numerous nations preaching and teaching had come to serve on faculty at my institution. He

---

4. The topic of fasting will be briefly discussed in the summary of the book.

was known for his rugged approach to ministry and challenging statements. One such statement was a rather light-natured rebuke to missionary students who questioned the culinary characteristics of particular third-world countries. His response was quite simple, and yet poignant, "You're not going there to eat!" So also we are not here to eat! Our lives have a higher purpose and calling. This can be seen in Jesus's response to the first temptation, in which he quotes Deuteronomy 8:3, "One does not live by bread alone, but by every word that comes from the mouth of God." The popular statement, "You are what you eat," means that a human being is nothing more than a biological machine, a product of what is physiologically consumed. However, according to Jesus's quote of Deuteronomy 8:3, true human life is not in what one puts in one's mouth, but in what comes out of God's mouth! It is animals that live on the level of physical needs only. Human beings are to live on a higher plane. To be enslaved to inordinate desire for food and drink is to be animalistic and simple, whereas to put food in its proper perspective and live life as a servant of God and others is to be as Christ. Perhaps Luke's description of the temptation narrative is telling in that he begins the narrative by informing the reader that Jesus went into spiritual combat with the devil in the wilderness being "full of the Holy Spirit" (Luke 4:1). The contrast here is that whereas on the one hand Jesus is physically hungry, that is, *empty*, he is spiritually *full*. The challenge in life is to trade the satisfaction of physical fulfillment for the satisfaction of spiritual fulfillment. To satisfy one's hunger with the word and will of God, as the ancient sages told us, will assist one in overcoming food indulgence, gluttony, and over-eating.

The Sermon on the Mount is another important synoptic narrative for our concerns, and it has often been regarded as the most significant of all the teachings of Christ. Not only is it a long-sustained series of beautiful moral and ethical instructions, but its placement, particularly in the book of Matthew, is notable. Geographically speaking, Jesus is physically on an elevated place, thereby resembling a second coming of Moses, who was once himself on a mountain. Jesus is the new and greater Moses, redefining the Torah and inaugurating a new gift from God. His words in this sermon, although consistent with the Mosaic revelation, nonetheless supersede the Mosaic Law code. Also, the Sermon on the Mount is placed strategically within Matthew's gospel in that it is the first lengthy teaching of Jesus. It is an epochal event, thereby launching a new era of human history—the coming of the Kingdom of God. There are a handful of places in the Sermon on the Mount where food and eating are mentioned that we shall explore.

The first mention of food and eating in the Sermon on the Mount is in the famous beatitudes. Jesus said, "Blessed are those who hunger and thirst for righteousness, for they will be filled" (Matt 5:6). This sort of hungering and thirsting is the kind that we have been speaking of in the preceding paragraphs, where spirituality is in mind. For one to have the express desire for righteousness most likely represents the pursuit of a personal kind of holiness as well as a societal wholeness. That is, one should not be content to live in a world that is unfair and inequitable, for this certainly is the nature of the surrounding beatitudes of Matthew 5:3–12. Eschatologically speaking, the "have nots" will one day become the "haves," and the "haves" will become the "have nots," as in the story of the nameless rich man and Lazarus (Luke 16:19–31). Those who desire righteousness desire to always do the right thing concerning themselves and others. Such shall be "filled." They may lack in the present for an abundance of food and drink, but their future hope is a world made right by God. In the meantime, this is what they live and labor for. There is resonance with Micah 6:1–8, a passage previously discussed, where one recognizes that it is in the character of God not to hunger for food offerings and sacrifices but to hunger for kindness, justice, and humility to be practiced in society.

Luke's version of the Matthew 5:6 beatitude takes a slightly different slant, "Blessed are you who are hungry now, for you will be filled" (Luke 6:21). He especially emphasizes the rich/poor contrast here and in the surrounding beatitudes. This is consistent with the entire gospel of Luke, perhaps because he is a physician and perhaps because he is a Gentile. He adds woe statements to the rich (Luke 6:24) and to those who are well-fed: "Woe to you who are full now, for you will be hungry" (Luke 6:25). According to Luke, Mary, the mother of Jesus, had made a similar declaration in her famous Magnificat, "He has filled the hungry with good things, and sent the rich away empty" (Luke 1:53). In light of such statements by Jesus and Mary, it is difficult to want to live a lifestyle of the rich and over-fed. A theological approach to eating, diet, and weight control takes such matters into consideration and assists one in living a life of moderation.

Contained within the Sermon on the Mount is the most famous of all biblical prayers—the Lord's Prayer (Matt 6:9–13; Luke 11:2–4). As regards our concerns about food and God, Jesus makes the supplication within his prayer to "give us this day our daily bread." This simple request of Jesus can go a long way toward assisting us with a theological approach to food, eating, diet, and weight control. It is a prayer of the needy, not the greedy, an urgent and precious petition for those who live from hand to mouth. Life in antiquity was lived one day at a time, and the Israelites had especially experienced this during the wilderness wanderings (Exod 16:4). Laborers in the first century of the Common Era, that is, Jesus's day, oftentimes had to look for work on a daily basis and were typically paid at the end of every work day (Matt 20:1–8). Illness or inability to work would have meant disaster and ruin. To ask for "daily bread" is to ask for the ability to survive day to day and to learn to be trusting in God for provision. This lesson is clearly in view for the twelve disciples, as the Lord commissioned them on their ministry task to "take nothing for their journey except a staff; no bread, no bag, no money in their belts . . ." (Mark 6:8). If we fast forward to the modern-day western world, life obviously has changed much. I would not advocate that we go back to the ancient sort of daily fight for survival, but certainly something valuable is lost today because real dependency on God becomes more and more distant as we peer into full refrigerators[5] and perhaps growing bank accounts and investments for the future. The Lord's Prayer reminds us that we should pray daily and trust God for daily needs even when we have no worries about what we will eat for the day. In fact, our very ability to work and provide a living comes from God's hand!

Although Jesus taught that one is in need of God's daily provision, he also taught in the Sermon on the Mount that one should not be anxious for one's physical needs (Matt 6:25–34). In this section he teaches the value of life and the value of the individual, "Is not life more than food?" (Matt 6:25). This is an important question to meditate on. Yes, life is more than food! A proper theological mindset will once again provide one with the ability to put food in its proper perspective. Food is simply fuel that we need to accomplish our God-given tasks. We should not be anxious about food, whether it is having too little to eat or too much to eat, leading to weight problems. Our focus should be the life that God has given to us. Jesus makes comparison with the birds of the air, noting that if their physical needs are met, then so also shall the needs of his followers be met. He queries, "Are you not of more value than they?" (Matt 6:26). Yes, you are more valuable than the birds of the air, as well as the fish of the sea and the birds of the sky. In fact, many of the problems people face in life, such as food abuse, can be traced back to a poor self-image that can sneak in over time due to a variety of factors. But Jesus emphasized the "you" in Matthew 6:26. And this indeed means you!

5. See here especially Pollan, *The Omnivore's Dilemma,* chapters 18 and 19, where he records for us firsthand what it is to both hunt and gather our own food.

If we reach back to the creation theology of Genesis 1, we are reminded that God made humans in his own image (Gen 1:26–27). This should be the starting point for any proper theory of anthropology. That is, there is one creature on this planet that stands out far above all other things, and that is human beings, because they are created in the very image of the Almighty. The more people understand that they are designed beautifully and wonderfully by God (Ps 139:14), the more they will desire to not abuse their bodies with food or any other potentially abusive substance. Pagans,[6] however, "strive" for those things that are material (Matt 6:32). "Strive" here is rather intensive, meaning a strong craving and desire. But the follower of Christ's "striving" (from the same Greek root word) should be for the Kingdom of God (Matt 6:33). In a word, the Christian should have goals far beyond that which is material or physical. Rather than being absorbed by thoughts of food delights, Christians may at times be so focused that they have to remind themselves to eat so as to keep their bodies energized for whatever task may be at hand. Believers in Christ do not adopt a completely otherworldly view of economics and money, but they will assess their usefulness in relation to other more serious matters, such as the plight of the planet and deprivations of the poor. Tom Hafer states it this way:

> By broadening our mission from our personal weight issues to the health of the global community, we demonstrate compassionate wellness, and our personal weight issues become significantly less challenging. The switch from struggling with our own abundance to addressing the needs of our neighbors will awaken our deeper hunger that is not satisfied with food: the need to truly love our neighbor.[7]

6. This is the basic meaning of the word "Gentile" here. It is an irreligious person who fundamentally is a heathen.

7. Hafer, *Faith & Fitness*, 54.

Matthew, Mark, and Luke have provided us with some profound words and actions of Jesus regarding what it is to hunger as well as to think about food in ways that perhaps we have never thought before. The temptation in the wilderness and the Sermon on the Mount, as we have seen, are especially useful.

THE GOSPEL OF JOHN

The gospel of John provides a unique perspective of the life and ministry of Jesus, unlike what is seen in the three synoptics. The words and teachings of Jesus in this gospel provide a viewpoint of a divine Jesus who, arguably, is more intimate than what is seen in Matthew, Mark, and Luke. Eating bread and drinking water, for instance, are used on a number of occasions by Jesus in a metaphorical sense to teach a spiritual lesson—that being that true life can only be found by partaking in the life of Christ. Physical bread and water pass through the body, providing only a temporary purpose, but Christ gives eternal life to those who partake of his ways and teachings. This can be seen near the end of John's gospel in a post-resurrection event. In these days immediately following the death of Jesus the somewhat befuddled disciples had reverted back to their fishing trade. They seemed to think they had no recourse now that their master had apparently been taken from them. They were completely unsuccessful in their new attempt at an old way of life—that is, until Jesus appeared on the scene (John 21:1–6). Upon having such a great catch of fish, the disciples recognized that it was Jesus and therefore made their way to him (John 21:7–11). Jesus then made a short and simple request, "Come dine with me" (John 21:12 KJV). Outwardly, this might appear to be nothing more than a request to come and have fish for breakfast. But in reality the statement has a larger meaning consistent with the symbolic invitations to eternal life that are abundant in the gospel of John (e.g., John 3:5). This fourth gospel might indeed be summarized as a plea for the reader to "come and dine" with

Christ. The metaphor is used elsewhere in Johannine literature, such as the well-known verse:

> Listen! I am standing at the door, knocking; if you hear
> my voice and open the door, I will come in to you and
> eat with you, and you with me (Rev 3:20).

Eating gives life, and the spiritual metaphor for this is applied readily here in the book of Revelation as well as in the gospel of John. It is not surprising, then, that immediately following the shared breakfast Jesus instructs Simon Peter to take care of the believing community with the symbolism of "feeding" (John 21:15–17). The lessons to be applied for the purposes of this book are to realize that our longing and desire should be to join in the life of Christ. It is his very person that satisfies and makes whole. Physical food and drink are a temporary pleasure, serving a temporary purpose. We should view fellowship with Christ, be it prayer, study, worship, or any other spiritual discipline, as that which makes us complete. Fleshly pleasures, such as food consumption, cannot satisfy the longing and need of the human heart; only partaking of Christ by faith can!

There are two specific metaphors that Jesus uses in reference to himself in the gospel of John in regard to food and drink. The first is that Jesus speaks of himself as the provider of the "the water of life" and the second is that he is "the bread of life." The challenge for the reader or hearer is to "hunger and thirst" (John 6:35) for this bread and water.

Water figures early in the text of the gospel of John in a spiritual sense, such as in the wedding of Cana (John 2:1–11) and the conversation with Nicodemus (John 3:1–21). But nowhere does Jesus employ the metaphor more obviously than in his encounter with the woman of Samaria (John 4:7–45). She is a timeless figure, representative of the typical human being who is almost exclusively concerned with material provision and not so much the welfare of her soul. Jesus having conversation alone with a woman might have been viewed as scandalous, but the fact that she is a woman of questionable character (five husbands and presently living with a man who is not her husband [John 4:18]) intensifies the context. Add to this that she is a Samaritan, a people who had a historic racial and religious division with pure Jews like Jesus, and the overall milieu of the encounter becomes somewhat radical. Jesus's disciples were astonished that he was in conversation with this woman (John 4:27). In fact, a few of the Genesis narratives record romantic encounters between a man and a woman who is a stranger taking place at wells: Isaac (via a servant) and Rebekah (Gen 24:10–27) and Jacob and Rachel (Gen 29:1–12). One could add Moses and Zipporah to this list also (Exod 2:15–21).

There is no hint of Jesus being allured romantically or sexually to the Samaritan woman, as he shows himself again and again to be spiritually minded in the encounter. A few chapters later in the gospel of John we read of Jesus being left alone with a woman of obvious loose sexual morals; however, there was no room for Jesus to think of selfish sexual desires, as he quickly taught the lesson and then sent her on her way (John 8:1–11). It was discussed in the previous chapter of this book that some of the theologians of the church have made connections between lust for food and lust for sex. One who cannot gain control over inordinate urges for food and drink is not likely to gain control over other inordinate physical urges, such as sex in an immoral context. The Old Testament has provided plenty of examples of men, especially powerful men, being brought down by inability to control their sexual appetite. Samson and David especially come to mind. In an age of Internet pornography, pop songs that are almost exclusively about romantic love and sexuality, and general vice offered at almost any juncture, men particularly need to control their physical desires. Much can be accomplished by starting with the stomach.

For Jesus in John 4, not only is a sexual encounter clearly the last thing on his mind, but he also does not even appear to be concerned with the so-called Samaritan defilement. His focus is on attempting to lift this woman's level of thinking from material needs to spiritual realities, and he will do this by tactfully turning the water of a literal well into a spiritual lesson. He offers her "living water" (John 4:10). It is not a great stretch of the imagination, for Jews had always considered that the Torah is a water of life. The connotation of "living water" would have meant water that is in motion, like the running water of a stream or river. It is water that is generally pure and clean. The early Christians would later on prefer baptism in such waters. I have oftentimes taught my young son that in a wilderness survival situation he should drink water from the place in the stream where the water is moving most rapidly, for that is the cleanest water to draw from. As far as the woman at the well was concerned, the term "living water" would have initially meant to her fresh spring water, such as the well supplied. She could not understand Jesus's statement, for he had no means to draw this so-called "living water" from the well. She would have gladly welcomed a way to get water without having to make the long, hot trip from the village. She may even have thought that Jesus was speaking of using some sort of magical formula to create water. But Jesus was of course not speaking of "magic water," just as there are no magical formulas for weight control today, even though many are marketed. All in all, she failed to comprehend, just as Nicodemus had (John 3:10) and just like we oftentimes do.

What Jesus offered was not magic but "the gift of God" (John 4:10). It is a special term here, emphasizing not presents given by men but an expression of divine bounty. He was offering her eternal life. Ponce De Leon, and others, may have pursued a fountain of youth in their search to live forever, but what Jesus offers is not fantasy. The more one longs for Jesus as the very water of life, the less one needs to concern oneself with the material world, and the less one is consumed with thoughts of food and drink. This is made obvious as the narrative of John 4 continues. Jesus's disciples were urging him to eat, as he no doubt was famished and physically exhausted from the rigors of ministry (John 4:31, 33). Even so, his response was, "I have food to eat that you do not know about . . . My food is to do the will of him who sent me and to complete his work" (John 4:32, 34). If our food is as Jesus, that is to do the will and the work of the Father, and if we can condition ourselves to think about food theologically, as Jesus did, we can gain the upper hand when it comes to overindulgence in food. As was stated earlier, I am not in this world to eat, but I am in this world to do the will and work of my heavenly Father. This proper theological approach will help me to maintain a modest balance of food consumption and will assist me in diet and weight control. Good theology leads to good practice; bad theology leads to bad practice.

The imagery of living water is also used by Jesus in John 7. The context is the Jewish Festival of Tabernacles. Jews would gather for a number of days in makeshift booths to commemorate the forty years of wilderness wanderings experienced by their ancestors in the days of Moses. Those days were days when food and water were scarce. The Israelites living in Canaan, however, had usually enjoyed regular rainfall and plentiful crops. The Feast of Tabernacles celebration that Jesus was experiencing included a daily procession of priests walking from the temple to the pool of Siloam, from which they drew water that was poured out as a libation at the altar. This was accompanied by the recital of Isaiah 12:3 "With joy you will draw water from the wells of salvation." There are other salvific allusions to water in the Old Testament as well (e.g., Isa 55:1; Ezek 47:9; Zech 14:8). Jesus had witnessed day after day this repetitive ritual, until finally, on the last day of the feast, at a climactic moment, he seemingly could take the pageantry no more. He cried out:

> Let anyone who is thirsty come to me, and let the one
> who believes in me drink. As the Scripture has said, "Out
> of the believer's heart shall flow rivers of living water"
> (John 7:37–38).

The interpretation to this saying is given in the following verse:

> Now he said this about the Spirit, which believers in him
> were to receive; for as yet there was no Spirit, because
> Jesus was not yet glorified (John 7:39).

Jesus was offering a new sort of water, as he did with the woman of Samaria. It is a contrast of the old and new, as he also taught in the wineskins lesson (Mark 2:22). The religion of the Jews was the old way, which now needed to make room for the new way inaugurated by Jesus Christ and the coming of the Holy Spirit. Jesus was requiring an individual response of faith rather than a collective observance of a ritual, which was really all the Feast of Tabernacles could be. The new supersedes the old, as it always does, whether it is in medicine, technology, or theology.

In considering the water analogies of John 4 and 7, I am reminded of the movers who helped my family and I move into our present home a few years back. After an exhausting and de-hydrating day, the many young men who had worked so hard asked for a drink of water, which my wife was happy to provide. She filled numerous glasses to the top from our tap and gave them cheerfully to the young men, only to watch them spit the stale well water out of their mouths. They were quite thirsty, yet in spite of this were not capable of swallowing the less-than refreshing water. They waited until they could find a store from which they could buy pure, bottled water. Even now I don't drink the well water from my tap but instead buy and drink bottled water. In a spiritual sense, what Jesus offers is the pure kind of religion that comes through a dynamic and living faith in him. The religion of the Jews, as all religion and human philosophical systems, is more like that well water that cannot satisfy. As we embrace the invitation of Jesus to drink from the "rivers of living water" that he offers, we find that life lived in him is what satisfies. A theological approach to life, with Jesus at the center of that life, assists one in understanding what it truly means to feast.

We have had a look at the metaphor of drinking water that gives life in the gospel of John. We now turn our attention to the metaphor of eating bread in this same gospel. This takes place particularly in chapter 6. Jesus speaks of himself as "the bread of life," and he invites others to not just eat of the bread he provides, as in the water of life, but to actually eat of him. His request becomes a bit more radical here. It is a curiosity to note that in the end, when Jesus is betrayed, Judas does so in the ironic act of eating bread with Christ (John 13:26).

Jesus's referring to himself as "the bread of life," which happens only in the gospel of John, takes place following his miraculous feeding of the multitude (John 6:1–14) and his walking on water (John 6:15–21). He was aware that the crowds followed him because he was able to provide them with food (John 6:26). He therefore challenged them, saying, "Do not work for the food that perishes, but for the food that endures for eternal life, which the Son of Man will give you . . ." (John 6:27). He appeared to be so disturbed by the multitudes longing to be fed that he actually ignored the disciples' question about when he arrived and went straight to his teaching point about the "food that endures for eternal life." It could easily be deduced, then, that the Lord was annoyed with temporal and material pursuits that lack any quest for the true eternal life that he provided through belief in him (John 6:29). A theological approach to food, eating, diet, and weight control is not obsessed with calories and carbohydrates, or carnal concerns whatsoever, but is fixed on a pursuit of Jesus himself and the life he offers.

As the narrative develops, a discussion about Moses and the manna provision during the wilderness wanderings takes center stage (John 6:31–65). The rabbis had expected and taught that the Messiah would cause bread to descend from heaven, as was seen in the days of Moses (John 6:30–31). Jesus's bold response to this expectation was that Moses was not the giver of true spiritual bread but that he himself was the only source for real living. Upon further questioning by the disciples, he went so far as to say, "I am the bread of life" (John 6:35), thereby placing himself above Moses and proclaiming himself to be Messiah. It is the first of a series of similar "I am" declarations made by Jesus found only in the gospel of John ("bread," 6:41, 6:48, 6:51; "light," 8:12; "door," 10:7; "good shepherd," 10:11; "resurrection and life," 11:25; "way, truth, and life," 14:6; "true vine," 15:1). These "I am" statements are an echo of Moses's encounter with God at the all-important burning-bush scene where God first revealed his name to Moses as "I am"[8] (Exod 3:14). Jesus clearly allowed that story to resonate again and again every time he referred to himself as "I am" something or other. For the Jews there could be no mistake about it, for the Greek of "I am" in the gospel of John is the same Greek construction as Exodus 3 in the Septuagint, the well-known Greek translation of the Old Testament.

The Jews were offended with this self-claim of Jesus and began to have debate and discussion about these things (John 6:41, 42, 52, 60, 66). As the narrative progresses, Jesus ups the ante, not only telling them that he is the bread of life but that indeed they had to also eat of his flesh and drink of his blood (John 6:53). This kind of cannibalistic talk was repulsive to the Jews, particularly the idea of drinking his blood. Throughout the first part of the passage the standard and expected Greek word for "eat" is used (John 6:26, 50, 51, 53). However, at one point near the end of the engagement Jesus switched verbs, using a term found in classical Greek that takes on the meaning of "partake" (John 6:54, 56, 57, 58). It connotes the kind of eating that has to do with munching, gnawing, or nibbling, often used of animals

8. From where we derive the Hebrew divine name "Yahweh."

eating. I recall a friend years ago bragging that he needed to continuously have something in his mouth to eat or chew on. I'm not
sure that he had much of a point to make, but the point that Jesus
appears to be making is that we should "chew on this," namely
that we must be partakers of his very being. We should dine with
him, and upon him, daily and continuously. The only time in the
latter part of this narrative that the verb for "eat" switches back
to the more common term is in John 6:58 when Jesus spoke of
the fathers in the day of Moses eating. Immediately following
this statement in this same verse Jesus once again switched the
verb to the more intimate "partake" kind of eating in reference
to one eating of Jesus to gain eternal life. Jesus was providing
every opportunity for the hearers to grasp and believe his message through his selective word choice.

Although his message of eating his flesh and drinking his
blood was figurative, nonetheless what he offered was real food
and drink, which produces real life in abundance. One can even
in the present chew or feed on Jesus in many different ways
through faith and belief in him. Study, prayer, meditation, worship, partaking of the Lord's supper, fellowship, hearing sermons
and lessons, and perhaps many other spiritual exercises can fall
under the category of "eating his flesh and drinking his blood."
The Christians of the early centuries were viewed as peculiar and
even cannibalistic by pagan Romans because of this kind of "eating flesh and drinking blood" talk. But to the one with insight
Jesus's meaning is spiritual (John 6:63) and engaged by faith and
discipleship. It is a free-standing invitation to eat and drink all
day long, 24/7, as it might be stated in modern vernacular! For
those of us who struggle with the allurement and temptation
of overindulgence in literal food and drink, leading to excess
weight and misery, let it be known that if our thinking about
food becomes increasingly theological, we can gain victory
through continuous partaking in the life of Christ. I am learning

to eat all day long, not the food that perishes, but the food that endures for eternal life!

The synoptic gospels gave us food for thought in the temptation in the wilderness and the Sermon on the Mount. The gospel of John has given us a portrayal of Jesus who offers bread and water, not the primitive prison diet variety, but living water and the bread of life! In him we have all we need to satisfy our souls. The more we can engage this with our minds and with our very lives, the more we will find that material things such as food and drink do not interest us as much as they once might have.

POINTS TO PONDER

1. Make good eating decisions daily!

2. You are not as hungry as you think you are!

3. Your body can endure more than you know!

4. Allow your body to be tested with hunger!

5. Hunger teaches dependence upon God!

6. Food denial prepares us for tasks!

7. You're not here to eat!

8. Live life in moderation!

9. Ask for "daily" bread!

10. Life is more than food!

11. Come dine with Christ!

12. Thirst for the water of life!

13. Hunger for the bread of life!

5

Food and Eating in the New Testament Church

THE LIFE and teaching of Jesus was embraced not only by his original disciples, but it was also eventually embraced by a significant number of Jews dispersed throughout the Roman Empire. This message of faith in Jesus as the Jewish Messiah spread to the Gentile world as well during what we now call the first century of the Common Era. Christianity had begun, and so had "the Church," which basically means "the called-out ones." Christianity grew stronger and stronger and became a force to be reckoned with. As Christianity grew, the distribution and sharing of food played an important role in providing definition to what it meant to be a part of the Christian community. In this chapter we shall explore how the first Christians understood the role of food in the sharing of their life of faith in Jesus as the Christ. Eating was a part of the fellowship of the Christian movement, and it also had significance regarding how Jews and Gentiles would relate to each other in this new merger of faith. Also, the partaking of what is now known as the Lord's Supper played, and should still play, a key role in Christians' thinking about food.

FOOD, FELLOWSHIP,
AND THE GENTILE MISSION

The Bible records the development of earliest Christianity in the book of Acts. This entity known as the Church was clearly launched in Acts 2 with the outpouring of the Holy Spirit during the Jewish festival of Pentecost. In a moment, the community of believers in Jesus multiplied to more than three thousand (Acts 2:41). Luke, the writer of the book of Acts, was certain to inform the reader that the breaking of bread and sharing food together in each other's homes was a foundational characteristic of this early Christian movement (Acts 2:42, 46). Just as an ordinary meal among Jews would have had something of a sacred flavor about it, so now the Christians, Jew and Gentile alike, would celebrate loving devotion to Jesus together in a typical environment of love, joy, and praise. The very phrase "breaking of bread" may have subtly connoted the passion of Christ, something we will say more about in the following section on the Lord's Supper.

By sharing food with each other, these Christians demonstrated, first, a celebrative attitude toward the new community formed through the death and resurrection of Christ, and second, a meeting of one another's basic human needs. In fact, we learn that the Christians sold their personal possessions to share all things in common, Barnabas being a leading example (Acts 2:42; 4:32–37). The context of early Acts is that many Jews who were living in the dispersion throughout the Mediterranean world had made the pilgrimage to Jerusalem for the Feast of Pentecost, but upon being converted to the message of Jesus, they stayed in the environs of Jerusalem to be trained and discipled in the new faith. This moment of massive Christian growth demanded that those of means help meet the needs of the sojourners who were temporarily away from home and livelihood. Also, an integral part of Jewish law had always been to show hospitality for the sojourner, stranger, or alien (Deut 10:19).

Standing among the earliest of New Testament books to be written was the book of James. This James was also a leader in the embryonic Church (Acts 15:13). One of the best-known passages of the New Testament, the faith and works passage (Jas 2:14–26), comes from this book. We see here that from the very earliest of Christian traditions the community of faith was to demonstrate its faith by meeting practical needs, particularly those things as obvious as food and clothing (Jas 2:15–16). Christians today who struggle with food self-indulgence oftentimes miss this important concept, that the giving and sharing of food is a way to express one's love for Christ. To exhibit behaviors such as getting up in the middle of the night to sneak food for oneself or to hide candy in secret compartments so as not to be seen eating it by others oftentimes reflects the theological shallowness of meeting one's own *wants*, without regard for the *needs* of others. The more we think about food as an opportunity to share in the life of Christ, be it when eating alone or with others, the less we will see food as an object of personal gratification.

The Apostle Paul said in his letter to the Church at Philippi:

> I know what it is to have little, and I know what it is to have plenty. In any and all circumstances I have learned the secret of being well-fed and of going hungry, of having plenty and of being in need (Phil 4:12).

The secret that Paul speaks of appears to be what he states in the following verse, "I can do all things through him who strengthens me" (Phil 4:13). His relationship with Christ gave him the ability to keep perspective in any circumstance. If he had much and was well-fed, he could celebrate Christ. If he had little and even went hungry, his faith in Christ allowed him to maintain a balance of thought. Paul was not the sort of person to be given to lust for food, and this is because of a deep, abiding spirituality and knowledge of Christ. If he had even the minimum amount of food and shelter required to sustain life, he understood how to be content (1 Tim 6:8). He commends the Christians at Philippi for assisting him materially during his lean times (Phil 4:14). In fact, he commends them all the more because they stood alone in this good deed of sharing in matters of basic human need (Phil 4:15). It is in this context that he is able to say, "And my God will fully satisfy every need of yours according to his riches in glory in Christ Jesus" (Phil 4:19). The more one is given to this Christ-like attitude, the less one will struggle with matters of food overindulgence, and for that matter, anything that might be a vice.

In returning to the story of the developing Church in the book of Acts, one discovers that matters of equal food distribution among widows became a problem (Acts 6:1). At the heart of this problem was division caused by diversity in race and language; for the Christians were becoming a melting pot of those who were more Greek influenced in culture and language and those who were more Jewish in orientation. The Greek-influenced believers had a complaint against the more Jewish believers, who apparently were receiving favoritism in the community. I am reminded of how Joseph once showed such favoritism to his full blood brother Benjamin by giving him five times more food than the other half-brothers (Gen 43:34). The Joseph/Benjamin story is a unique context, but the reality in today's world is that Americans and those in the first world are happy to consume the proverbial "five times more" food than the rest of the world. It is a shame that Westerners can be so focused on losing weight while so much of the world goes without and even starves. More than a billion people worldwide don't even know where their next meal will come from.[1] As early as 1960, America spent $500 million on food fads, extreme diets, and cure-alls.[2] America also produces enough food to provide nearly twice the amount of calories

1. Hafer, *Faith & Fitness*, 53.
2. Ibid, 53.

recommended by the United States Department of Agriculture (USDA) for every American.[3]

To illustrate our American plague, a friend recently told me of his visit to a Chinese all-you-can-eat buffet. His family loaded plate after plate of various foods, even as I know I habitually do in such restaurants. However, they were humbly challenged by observing the Chinese patrons who took very small amounts of food, which also happened to be the lighter, healthier kind. This in itself is a portrait of why America suffers from obesity where-as Far-Eastern cultures have minimal problems with it. There is an obvious inequity in the world, and a starting point for doing something about it is to change our individual eating habits. This same friend spoke of an acquaintance who weighs in at well over three hundred pounds, and I do not mean that much of it was muscle. This person came to a similar all-you-can-eat Chinese buffet and spent a lengthy portion of the day eating plate after plate after plate of food. Finally, the Chinese owner approached his very non-profitable, engrossed customer and asked him to take his money back, leave, and never come back again. What an act of public shame, although the eater in the story probably never gave a second thought to it!

Another rather humorous anecdote passed along to me came from an acquaintance of my wife. This acquaintance hum-bly tells of how, in the process of caring for an aging grandmother with Alzheimer's disease, she was constantly referred to as "the fat lady." This ailing grandmother, known for her meanness of spirit before her illness, spoke bluntly and honestly from a non-caring heart, not knowing that this person was indeed her own granddaughter-in-law. It is a shameful reflection of poor charac-ter and a not so well-lived life on the part of the aging woman, but her brutal honesty was a wake-up call to the young woman caring for her. Sometimes we need to be shocked before we take appropriate action! Weight gain is usually accomplished gradu-

3. Ibid, 52.

ally over a period of time, and we often are unable to recognize our worsening condition. We should not be surprised, then, to discover that weight loss will also need to take place over a period of time, through careful reflection and action.

The Church of Acts 6 resolved their inequitable food distribution problem by appointing deacons to attend to such matters. Material care for widows continued to be a concern for the Christian Church as it developed and organized (1 Tim 5). Theological thinking about food always has in mind the needs of the less fortunate and disadvantaged. I can still recall how as a young boy I used to offer a prayer at the family dinner table thinking I was repeating a prayer I thought I heard my parents would say, "Lord, please be with the missionaries in the *corn* fields." What they had in fact been saying in their prayers was, "Lord, please be with the missionaries in the *foreign* fields." I suppose there was something innocent about my thinking, as I somehow formulated in my mind that missionaries were in other countries helping the people to have enough corn and other crops to eat. Perhaps we still need to think this way, that we have a worldwide mandate and mission to help meet the needs of others in the world. True, there may be limitations to what I can do from a practical standpoint, but a proper theological approach to my personal eating, diet, and weight control will be an appropriate starting point and help me to live my life less selfishly, especially when it comes to how I approach food.

Speaking of missionaries, the Church of Acts eventually made its way out of Jerusalem and began its expansion to the world beyond. Although Greek-speaking Jews were a part of the Church (Acts 6) and Samaritan Jews became part of the Church (Acts 8), it was in Acts 10 that full-blooded Gentiles were invited to be participants. Interestingly enough, the outreach began with the Apostle Peter being hungry (Acts 10:10). God proceeded to give him a three-fold vision that revolved around animals to be eaten (Acts 10:11–16). The meaning of the vision became clear—

God had declared the Gentiles clean, and the time had come for them to hear the gospel of Jesus and be allowed to become partakers of the new faith (Acts 11:17–18). Peter's physical hunger took a backseat to God's evangelistic hunger, as he immediately attended to the mission the vision had evoked. By the end of Acts 10, Gentiles, once regarded as unclean by Jews, were now a part of the Christian faith. By the end of Acts 11, the Christian leaders in Jerusalem had accepted this new endeavor as the will of God. What remained to be resolved was the matter of which Jewish laws, food laws and others, were to be observed by Gentile converts to Christianity. This would become a primary concern at the first Christian council, which took place in Jerusalem and is recorded in Acts 15. But first, following Peter's success in proclaiming the Christian message to Gentiles, Barnabas and Saul (soon to be known as "Paul") were set apart by the Holy Spirit to go to distant regions as missionaries who would proclaim Christ's message to Jew and Gentile alike (Acts 13:2). The voice of the Holy Spirit was discerned here by food denial—that is, fasting. The result of this would be a tremendous influx of Gentile believers into the Church, the topic of Acts 13 and 14.

We return to the Jerusalem council of Acts 15. The most crucial issue at hand was the treatment of the Gentile converts. What aspects of Jewishness and Mosaic Law were these new brothers and sisters to keep? Food, which, as we have seen, has had certain restrictions in Jewish practice, would become a matter of debate. Did Gentiles need to observe the Jewish dietary practices? This, as well as other questions, would be of central focus for the growing Church. Ultimately, the libertarians, those with lenient policies toward Gentiles, would gain victory over the legalists, those with strict views regarding Gentile practice. The reason the question of food came up is because Jewish and Gentile Christians would have to eat together, and it was an expedient and practical matter of fellowship between the groups. The prevailing wisdom, captured in a letter by the council's leaders, was to provide a few guidelines for Gentile believers when it came to matters of eating:

> For it has seemed good to the Holy Spirit and to us to impose on you no further burden than these essentials: that you abstain from what has been sacrificed to idols and from blood and from what is strangled and from fornication. If you keep yourselves from these, you will do well. Farewell (Acts 15:28–29).

In sum, the restrictions were probably nothing more than a request for Gentile converts to stay away from gluttony and pagan diners that offered meat from animals that have not been drained of their blood and that were offered as sacrifice to pagan deities. These diners oftentimes provided lodging as well, which might make use of prostitutes who would provide "entertainment" to the traveler. These kinds of practices would obviously be offensive to a Jew, although they were perhaps somewhat standard practices in the business and commerce of the pagan world. Gentile Christians were simply being asked to avoid these places. The main point was for them to not give offense to their Jewish brothers and sisters who abhorred such heathen practices. This then became a primary tenet of New Testament Christianity, the need to preserve harmony and avoid giving offense, especially in matters of table fellowship.

Ironically, Peter, the very apostle who was the first to preach the message of salvation to Gentiles, became a violator of this principle of equality and harmony in table fellowship. Paul rebuked him for being double-minded in his policies (Gal 2:11). Peter was happy to initially eat with fellow Gentile believers—that is, until more conventional Jews associated with James came, at which time he withdrew himself from his Gentile brothers to associate only with those who were Jewish (Gal 2:12). This was a great hypocrisy that influenced others as well, even one as noble and great as Barnabas (Gal 2:13). Paul was strong and determined in his rebuke (Gal 2:14). He would later write to the Colossian church to let no one act as their judge in matters of eating (Col 2:16–23), and he regarded all food as good and acceptable from God (1 Tim 4:1–5). The writer of Hebrews said that the vegetation was blessed by God (Heb 6:7–8). James could view pretty much everything, including food, as a "perfect gift" of God (Jas 1:17), and he spoke of "precious crop from the earth" (Jas 5:7), and of the earth having "yielded its harvest" (Jas 5:18). Paul proclaimed that God was the maker of all things (Acts 17:24) and the one who supplied seed to the sower and bread for food (2 Cor 9:10). Paul's theology, like the theology of Genesis 3, was that we should work to pay for our food (2 Thess 3:7–12), so as to avoid disharmony.

There are two notable sections in the New Testament where Paul specifically addresses the issue of food to be eaten and table fellowship. They are, first, Romans 14 and on into 15, and second, 1 Corinthians 8 and following. In both situations, the concern has to do with eating meat that had been sacrificed to idols. Most of the meat that was sold in the marketplace in Paul's day had been offered to idols in the pagan temples first. It was very difficult to know for sure whether meat in any given shop had been part of a sacrifice. Also, it was an accepted social practice to have meals in a temple or in some place associated with an idol.[4] To have nothing to do with such gatherings was to cut oneself off from social interaction with others.[5] During my one year of study in England, a friend stated that the English social custom was a "pub culture," meaning that social intercourse took place at pubs, over drink for sure and possibly food as well. To be part of the culture meant to be willing to meet with people in the English pubs. This has certain similarities to the world of Paul's day, with the one notable difference of the presence of meat sacrificed to idols.

4. Morris, "1 Corinthians," 120.

5. Ibid, 120.

Contemporaries of Paul who were Jewish Christians would have especially had issues with the meat sacrificed to idols. Sharing a meal with Gentile believers was problematic for these more strict observant Jewish types because they could never be fully sure of the history of the meat they might be eating. Had the meat been a part of a pagan temple or ritual? Had a pagan priest handled the meat and offered it to an idol? The question for Paul was a matter of conscience and whether one should even make a fuss or seek to know how a meat was handled. For him, a Christian was at perfect liberty to eat meat of any kind (1 Cor 8:8) and shouldn't ask questions (1 Cor 10:27). However, he knew quite well that many other Christians, especially those with Jewish heritage, were not as emancipated as he was regarding this and other issues. He repetitively in his correspondence uses the terms "weak and strong" (Rom 14:1; 15:1; 1 Cor 8:7–12), the strong being those of clear conscience like himself and the weak being those inhibited by legalistic tendencies. Nonetheless, he has equal concern for both schools of thought, with a special plea for the strong to be patient with the weak (Rom 14:1–4, 10, 13; 15:1, 7; 1 Cor 8:9). There was no need for argumentation and debate on the matter, for it was not an issue of eternal life and eternal damnation. Paul's primary concern was preserving the unity of the faith. Jewish Christians and Gentile Christians needed to live together in harmony, without quarrelling and dividing over lesser matters, such as the food one ate. It was more important to see the act of sharing food as representative of sharing their lives together in the unifying faith that Jesus Christ established for all peoples.

In referring back once again to my overseas experience in England, I was privileged to be a part of an international Christian community during my stay there. We all lived together in university housing among many internationals, including a large contingency of Arab Muslims. We Christians were actually the minority and therefore encouraged one another consistently by sharing meals together. In fact, my wife and I successfully attempted to share many meals with Muslim families as well, which was a tremendously valuable learning experience. It probably was one of the greatest experiences of my Christian faith. One of my dear Chinese Malaysian Christian friends, the same one who had said I had a "big nose" in reference to a cold, instructed me to watch how people ate. It was his wisdom and humility that really instituted within me an awareness of how improperly I approached the table.

The primary point is that eating food in a selfless manner, with an eye toward the health of the community, is a vital part of a proper theological approach to eating, diet, and weight control. This might mean the worldwide community, as we have previously stated, it might mean individual family units, or it might mean larger social gatherings. Observing numerous church and other social functions over the years that have involved sharing meals together in one context or another has at times sickened me as I noticed first my own behavior and then the behavior of others. Cutting in line and the rush to be the first to eat, taking enormous quantities, especially when it is obvious that there is not enough to go around, getting in line for seconds when some have not yet eaten, and wasting food are just a sampling of less than godly behavior when it comes to eating in a corporate situation. Consider the words of Paul in Romans 14:17, "For the kingdom of God is not food and drink but righteousness and peace and joy in the Holy Spirit."

On the personal side of the eating matter Paul was a libertarian. He was free to eat whatever he wanted without violating his religious conscience. However, his ethos when it came to his body was rigorous and disciplined. In the midst of his discussions on the food sacrificed to idols issue he states, "But I punish my body and enslave it, so that after proclaiming to others I myself should not be disqualified" (1 Cor 9:27). The New American Standard Bible translates the word "punish" as "buffet" here. On a humorous note, I have preached the meaning of "buffet" as, rightly so, to "beat, bruise, or batter," as opposed to how some might like to pronounce and interpret it as the French word "buffet," meaning "restaurant" or "table." Paul was not saying, "I eat all that I want when I want"; he was saying quite the opposite. In referring back a few chapters in 1 Corinthians, Paul quotes, and then nullifies a common maxim, "Food is meant for the stomach and the stomach for food" (1 Cor 6:13). The larger issue at hand was that the Corinthians, strongly influenced by pagan thinking, felt that they were to satisfy their physical bodies, even if it meant engaging in immoral sexual pleasure. They reasoned that they might as well go ahead and satisfy their natural bodily functions, for that is what they are there for. They felt the same way about food, thinking something like, "I have a stomach, so I might as well fill it with all the food I want." Paul argued against this kind of thinking, postulating instead that such an attitude is not beneficial (1 Cor 6:12) and that the body houses the presence of God (1 Cor 6:19–20). The Corinthians needed a shift in their thinking, and we who would desire to control ourselves when it comes to eating do as well.

THE LORD'S SUPPER

Paul's discussion of the food sacrificed to idols that begins in 1 Corinthians 8 is really a continuation of his attempt to bring the divided church at Corinth back together. A division among the Corinthian congregation is the basic concern of the book (1 Cor 1:10–11). The eating issue extends over a number of chapters, leading to the issue of how the Corinthians partook together of the Lord's Supper (1 Cor 11:17–34). This practice is now recognized by almost all Christian traditions as a sacrament or ordinance and goes by a variety of names: Eucharist, Holy Communion, the Lord's Supper, and others as well. We have chosen to use the name the Lord's Supper because this is the phrase Paul uses in the biblical text (1 Cor 11:20). It was common custom in the ancient world for groups of people to meet together for meals. As Christianity developed, the various communities of faith would regularly celebrate a public feast known as a "love feast" (Jude 12). The Greek word for love is *agape*, a term that became almost uniquely Christian and that defined the fellowship of those who shared the hope in Jesus. It represented a God kind of love of the highest order. At these love feasts individuals would bring some food to a central place for dining, after which all would partake together of the whole. No member of Christ's followers was rejected from the meal, regardless of social class, and there was to be plenty of food for all. After feasting there was a special remembrance of the Lord's sacrificial death, symbolized in the eating of bread (Christ's body) and drinking from the cup (Christ's blood).

But in Corinth, problems had developed with this practice. Those who arrived to the meal first ate and drank to the point of drunkenness, while others went away from the community meal hungry (1 Cor 11:21–22, 33–34). Most likely, the wealthier believers brought a majority of the food, but they also were the ones consuming the majority of the food. The poorer believers among the community would have had to work longer at their jobs and with less freedom and therefore may have been late to the gathering. The result was that these lower-class citizens in Roman society continued to be treated and regarded as lower-class citizens in the Christian society, the very thing that the shared meal was to eliminate. The Jesus community was to be egalitarian, but the agape feast revealed the distinctions that were continuing to be made (1 Cor 11:17–18).

As it was in the Corinthian love feasts, so it is in our present world: those with means tend to be gluttons while those with less go hungry. Millions of Christians partake of the Lord's Supper monthly and even weekly, and yet there may be little thought given as to how much one has, indicated often by the amount we eat and drink, when so many in the world have so little. Paul warns that the Supper can be approached in an "unworthy manner" (1 Cor 11:27) and with dire consequences (1 Cor 11:29–30). Part of eating unworthily is a self-centered gluttony that takes no thought of the plight of others. The Christian agape meal was to be an expression of unity and fellowship for all people, breaking down the distinctions that are commonly made according to race, culture, and social status. The Christians were a new family, God's family, and celebrating the agape feast and the Lord's Supper was an indication of this. Families eat together.

In fact, eating together is one of the surest ways of expressing family ties and friendship. In America, one of the best-known portraits of the infancy of the nation, especially popular around our modern Thanksgiving time, are the stories and paintings of pilgrims eating with Native Americans. Although the eventual historical realities may have been somewhat different than peace and harmony, it is a picture of humans sharing in their common humanity. Sharing food can cross the boundaries that typically divide us as humans. Gillian Feeley-Harnik has produced an anthropological book on food. She states, "Subtle differences in social class—real or aspired to—may be marked by differences in food. Castes, occupational and religious groups, even whole nations, are distinguished by the food they eat."[6] If we are to be people who cross these boundaries, especially with an eye toward extending the family of God, then we should learn to eat the food of others, even if it is strange to us. In the midst of Paul's discussion of the food eaten in the Corinthian Church, he reminds them that he is willing to do whatever he has to do to win folks to the gospel of Christ (1 Cor 9:19–23), even in matters of eating (1 Cor 10:27, 33).

I recently returned from a vacation where I had opportunity to visit Walt Disney's Epcot Center. The theme park is characterized by a world showcase that has numerous foreign restaurants

6. Feeley-Harnik, *The Lord's Table*, 11. For a psychological approach to the same issue, see Logue, *The Psychology of Eating and Drinking*.

staffed with native citizens from the various nations represented. The food is of course a genuine and authentic display of that particular nation's culinary practices. It was a curiosity for me to observe English tourists attending the English pub, Irish tourists frequenting the Irish pub, Japanese visitors eating in the Japanese restaurant, and so on and so forth. Now perhaps these folks had been away from their respective home countries for some time and desired a taste of home. This is certainly understandable. But in a larger sense, the habit of migrating to the familiar, specifically in matters of food and eating, is a portrait of the division of the human family and the basic discomfort we have with those who are different from us. The Lord's Table and Christian agape feasts were and are to be a loud shout out against this type of practice and thinking. Learning to eat the food of others is a first step, among others, in global reconciliation and extending Christ's family worldwide. On the one hand, the numerous cultures in the world have given us a plethora of food types and delectables to enjoy, but on the other hand, human behavior is such that it tends to think, experience, and even eat narrow mindedly.

One of the novelties of the United States as a nation is its melting-pot mentality. It is represented by a multitude of ethnicities, races, and even religions. It is beautiful to witness the peaceful and harmonious cross-cultural sharing that often takes place among neighbors of these sub-cultures, particularly when it comes to eating with each other. However, it is equally disturbing when racism and narrow-mindedness reveal themselves through retreating to one's own culture and culinary practices exclusively. One of the fond memories I have of my mother is during the dinner hour when I was growing up. As a kid, I might have put up a fuss about the variety of foods she presented before me, of which certain items mandatory eating was applied. However, upon reflection in my adult years, I now value the exposure to food of all kinds of people groups and perhaps more importantly, to witnessing and experiencing the variety of God's creation in matters of food. When given opportunity, if you can indulge my use of modern sayings for the moment, we should attempt to "walk in the shoes of others" for "variety is the spice of life." Or better yet, let me rewrite the modern axiom, changing it from "walk in the shoes of others" to "eat with the forks/chopsticks of others."

I am reminded again of my one year as a student living in England, surrounded by a community of other international students. In the process of sharing dinner, or "tea," with students from twenty-eight nations in almost the same amount of days, I once ate what was called "sausage" with friends from a nation much different from the United States. My wife and I could swear to this day that this "sausage" was some sort of animal intestine, which quite frankly, and crudely, tasted and smelled as if what is housed in intestines was still present in the "food." Now my wife had creatively learned the art of spreading leftover food around a plate to make it look like much had been eaten. I lacked in this craft and therefore had to look for other means of escape, such as a hungry and willing family pet or a conveniently located waste basket. What horror my wife and I experienced as our foreign hosts attempted to put more and more on our plates, regardless of our polite replies of being well satiated. And the children of our hosts, well they treated this "sausage" like our kids would have treated ice cream or some other American sweet or delicacy. Nonetheless, I did my best, keeping in mind that a theological approach to eating necessitated that I did not eat food for the sake of my own satisfaction but for a larger purpose—God's purpose. The context at hand was one of outreach for the sake of friendship, and if possible, evangelism.

Anyhow, families eat together, and families have parties together. Tom Wright, in his *The Meal Jesus Gave Us: Understanding Holy Communion*, articulates in a creative fashion that the Lord's Supper is basically a party where the re-defined family of Christians is celebrating their unity in Jesus Christ.[7]

7. Wright, *The Meal Jesus Gave Us*, 5.

He discusses how parties have great symbolism, such as other cultural phenomena might. For instance: a handshake, waves, kisses, salutes, or raising a glass to toast all have unique but powerful meanings. Just as a birthday party carries the symbolism of bringing the past into the present, that is, the memory of the day of one's birth coupled with the present moment of that life and the hope of a great future for that life, so also the Lord's Supper joins the Jewish feast of Passover with Christ's Last Supper and the Church's present mission. The bread and cup of the Lord's Supper, shared differently in the variety of Christian traditions, are important and powerful symbols of Christ's sacrificial death and the mandate to be as Christ. In other words, food elements have become one of the greatest symbols of what Christianity is all about. The desecration of symbols—be they items as diverse as military medals, flags, tombstones, family heirlooms, marriage licenses, or wedding videos—is not well tolerated by society as a whole. Since food, in the form of the bread and cup, is a crucial symbol of Christianity, it is my desire to not desecrate this symbol by treating food as an object of self-indulgent pleasure. This is learning to think theologically about how we eat.

Markus Barth, son of famed twentieth-century Swiss theologian Karl Barth, writes of another kind of symbolism in the Lord's Supper. He sees the meal as "a framework of proclamation."[8] He of course takes this from Paul's statement, "For as often as you eat this bread and drink the cup, you proclaim the Lord's death until he comes" (1 Cor 11:26). He notes how Christian worship and practice tends to be predominately oral. Christians pray, sing, read aloud, recite creeds, preach homilies, speak testimonies, quote the Lord's prayer, and perhaps perform a whole host of other oral activities. Interestingly, the Lord's Supper is also oral. Believers place the bread and the contents of the cup in their mouths. It is a symbol and a reminder that the Christian shouts out loud to the world in a variety of ways that all people

8. Barth, *Rediscovering the Lord's Supper*, 54.

can be a part of the family of God by faith in the gospel of Jesus. Proclamation is important. Speaking is important. Conversation is important. The Jesus meal is basically a proclamation and an invitation to conversation. The Lord's Supper, the foundational family meal of the Jesus family, serves as a model for any family or group eating together. There should be proclamation and conversation when we eat with family and friends. How amiss it is when the stoic and rigid father demands utter silence from his young children at the dinner table under the guise of peace and control! Meals are a time to celebrate, talk, and share in meaningful conversation.

I grew up the youngest of four brothers, of which we were no more than five years apart from oldest to youngest. We experienced many noisy but pleasant dinner hours. My father used to say, "Let's talk ideas." My brothers and I would joke about it, but once again, as I matured, I could see the wisdom behind his request. The shared meal is the perfect time to commune with one another and to advance our understanding of things, particularly Christ and his kingdom. God had once upon a time commanded the ancient Israelites in the sharing of the Passover meal to not only eat, but also to tell or speak of the story of redemption from slavery. This was all done for the purpose of remembrance of this key event (Exod 12:26–27). In a similar fashion, Jesus charged his disciples at the Last Supper that when they ate and drank of it, they were doing it as an act of remembrance (Luke 22:19). Eating in general is more than just an act of self-preservation; it carries tremendous significance, symbolism, and remembrance. When food is shared with friends and family, there can and should be mutuality in eating, speaking, and remembering.

Oftentimes the Lord's Supper as practiced in the modern churches has little or no relation to eating and drinking outside the church walls. Arthur C. Cochrane, in his ethical approach to eating and drinking, states:

> With the problems of poverty and hunger, and of the production, distribution, and consumption of food, which oppress all people in their daily lives, it has virtually nothing to do. The Lord's Supper has no relation to people's work, their economics, and their politics. Moreover, it has no connection with the countless ways in which men and women eat and drink.[9]

Cochrane sees an unnecessary separation between the "sacred and secular"[10] here and reminds us of Paul's statement, "So, whether you eat or drink, or whatever you do, do everything for the glory of God" (1 Cor 10:31). In fact, this statement of Paul's might be the most useful biblical passage we have in directing us toward living our eating life in a proper theological manner. It might be worth memorizing. Cochrane would urge us, as Tom Hafer and others have done, to approach food and drink with a larger worldview in mind. Remember the hungry. Remember the oppressed. Henri M. Nouwen, in the very first statement of his book, *With Burning Hearts*, states, "Every day I celebrate the Eucharist."[11] This is a wonderful thing to do. I appreciate his approach to life, although I would suggest that we all pursue a less liturgical and less literal observance, though certainly that has its place, in the hopes of realizing that the bread and cup of Christ will reach out in a secular way as much they do in a sacred way. *The Book of Common Prayer* of the Anglican Church of Canada has a section on prayers and sayings for Holy Communion. One line states, "Feed on him in thy heart."[12] As we feed on Christ in the partaking of the Lord's Supper we should have greater awareness, concern, and action for our world at large.

The sacred points in the direction of the secular, but then the secular points back to the sacred. That is to say that when I

9. Cochrane, *Eating and Drinking with Jesus*, 8.

10. Ibid, 8.

11. Nouwen, *With Burning Hearts*, 11.

12. Smith, *A Holy Meal*, 83.

partake of Christ's supper, I am prompted to partake of a mission to the world. But as the world has its needs met through the mission of Christ's family, the world ultimately recognizes that common acts of eating and drinking are a symbol of their need for the eternal food Christ offers. As the masses of the world are fed, they in turn come to understand that what they really need is the food and drink that only Christ can offer, the true spiritual food spoken so much of in John's gospel. They no longer eat and drink merely for physical sustenance and survival, but they begin to long for the eternal life that only Jesus provides. It is in essence, although it sounds somewhat oxymoronic, a wonderful, vicious circle. The Jesus family comes together to share the Lord's Supper in a sacred way, which prompts action toward the needs of a secular world. The secular world, as its needs are met, becomes part of the Jesus family, and the Jesus family in turn partakes of the Lord's Supper. The Jesus family then enters into world mission, and on and on it goes, a world community growing in Christ in a positive way.

POINTS TO PONDER

1. Prefer the needs of others to your wants!

2. Think of the less fortunate when you eat!

3. Seek harmony in table fellowship!

4. Eat foods from different ethnicities!

5. The Communion elements are food—therefore, do not abuse food!

6. Seek meaningful conversation at the table!

7. Eat with a view toward world mission!

Summary

Digesting It All

We have attempted in this book to provide a fresh approach to the problem of food over-consumption in the United States and the Western world that has caused much of these societies to grow fat and unhealthy. A new way of thinking provided by theology in the Christian tradition can assist those who struggle with personal weight issues, whether they are gross obesity, gluttony, slight weight gain, or even eating with too little thought. This personal journey of a search for self-improvement and spirituality in matters of eating, diet, and weight control is an invitation for you, the reader, to come on the journey also, a journey that can be life-changing as we attempt to shift our thinking from self-indulgent dining in the flesh to a more self-sacrificial and contemplative dining in the spirit.

The biblical revelation introduces from the outset that God had prepared for humankind's need for food before humans were even created. The dry land and soil with their reproductive powers are God's gift to this, his most precious creation, which was created in his very image. Yet the few eating restrictions that were placed upon the first man and woman were violated in the garden of temptation, leaving humanity destitute and in a fallen state. Food and eating were central to the temptation and failure event. The mortality and suffering of humankind for all peoples can theologically be traced back to this, even our weight and health problems. From this point on food would have to be harvested from the soil with great difficulty, something that now seems far removed from day-to-day life for the typical person in today's Western culture.

The ancient Israelites of the Old Testament had to labor hard for their food, even though their history was marked at times by God's supernatural provision. Although hunting and gathering had eventually given way to farming, life was still hard. Work was hard, and food was simple. Hospitality was an expectation because traveling and the more common nomadic way of life were rigorous and treacherous. Stranger providing for stranger could be a matter of life and death. The Israelites made provision for such sojourners in their law code and even had developed an elaborate set of food laws and dietary restrictions. These laws and restrictions provided some protection against poor diet and unhealthy culinary practices, but above all, they might simply have been a theological statement, a statement that proclaims that there is uncleanness everywhere, water, earth, and sky, as there are unclean animals in all three of these elements. This might have been a reminder that the effects of sin are everywhere and that human survival depends upon the grace and intervention of God. They were to make certain food choices, and in so doing, they were to choose the holy over against the profane. How one ate was related to spirituality and holiness.

Israel's sages, as well as the sages of other cultures, took an interest in how one ate, relating it to moral virtue and spirituality. Gluttony is especially discussed in literature and theology. The medieval Christian Church considered it to be one of the notorious seven deadly sins, and the effect of gluttony is at present a leading cause of preventable death in the United States. The Church has defined gluttony as being expressed in five distinct ways: eating too soon, eating too delicately, eating expensively, eating greedily, and eating too much. Gluttony is distinctively non-Christian in so much that Jesus's call to discipleship was a call to self-denial. Three Old Testament case studies (i.e., Esau, Eglon, and Eli) on gluttony of different sorts were presented in our study. Their relationship to food and fatness as revealed in story form reflect negatively on their character and spirituality. They are in essence models of how not to behave when it comes to food and eating.

There are numerous teachings and actions involving food in the life and ministry of Christ. Two of the most notable of these are the temptation in the wilderness and the Sermon on the Mount. The temptation in the wilderness showed Jesus to be God's obedient Son, unlike Israel's unfaithfulness in the forty years of wilderness wanderings during Moses's day. The most fascinating comparison, however, is with Adam. Whereas Adam failed to be obedient to God, demonstrated in eating that which he should not have, Jesus showed his obedience by being willing not to eat the bread of temptation. Jesus modeled for us that food denial can prepare us for life's tasks and that we should seek to satisfy the spiritual self above the physical self. In his Sermon on the Mount he taught that our true hunger and thirst should be for righteousness and that we should not be anxious concerning material things, such as food. Rather, we should be thankful for daily provision and opportunity. The gospel of John in particular extends an invitation to dine with Jesus in ways that are far beyond the physical, offering us the privilege of partaking of Jesus himself. He is indeed the very bread of life who also offers living water for all. Our true food therefore is not primarily from the five major food groups, but it is to seek and desire to do the will of the Father. Perhaps Maslow's hierarchy of needs should be rearranged to put need for the life of Jesus before anything else.

Christianity was born in the coming and departure of Jesus from the world. As Christianity grew, the distribution and sharing of food played an important role in providing definition to what it meant to be part of the Christian community. Sharing meals was an act of celebrating the new Jesus family. It was also a way to meet one another's needs and express love and toleration to the new extended and culturally mixed family, of which Jesus himself was the head. The Lord's Supper was a particular act of sharing food together that was not just a celebration of God's family in Christ but also a proclamation, a shout-out, if you will, to the entire world of the unity that is shared by those who hold Christ in common, even if they have very little else in common, such as culture and ethnicity. The bread and cup are powerful Christian symbols, and because they are food items, one should not want to abuse or desecrate food in any manner (e.g., food fights, food waste, eating competitions, over-eating, etc.). Eating the Lord's Supper should provide one with a worldview that has in mind the greater good of all humankind. This means that over-eating should take a backseat to one's desire to be more modest and temperate in matters of food intake as one considers a world that suffers much from hunger and hardship. Eating should be done with God and the world in mind. To quote Saint Paul, "So, whether you eat or drink, or whatever you do, do everything for the glory of God" (1 Cor 10:31).

There are a number of other issues that could be mentioned in regard to thinking theologically about food, eating, diet, and weight control. Take, for instance, fasting. Fasting is a spiritual discipline, which is not for the faint of heart but for those who are serious about seeking God and controlling their physical appetites. It was a very common practice for the ancient Israelites as a nation, as well as for many Old Testament men and women of God (e.g., Moses, Elijah, Esther). Fasting is a denial of food and perhaps water, observed for any particular period of time. There are partial fasts (e.g., vegetables or fruit juice only) and there are more extreme fasts (e.g., many days of going without food, or no food and water for a few days). Fasting is observed for religious purposes and is not unique to Christianity. It should not be associated with hunger strikes or diets, both of which serve a different purpose. A religious or spiritual fast involves not only training the body but the training of the mind and heart as well. By setting apart time for fasting, be it a partial fast or an extreme fast or be it for one day or many, we momentarily set aside the material world we live in and try to capture the often-neglected spiritual side of life. Just as the Sabbath was once observed by the Hebrews as a way of ceasing from physical labor so as to focus on intangibles, such as time, eternity, spirituality, and God, so also fasting assists us to think about other matters. By denying the body we make room for the spirit and mind. Fasting frees up time, thereby allowing us to spend more time in study, service, or other acts of spiritual devotion. Persons in the biblical world fasted to humble themselves before God, to repent of sins, and to show an attitude of watchfulness. In general, such food denial was an act of willful suffering for the purposes of self-denial and expressing sorrow.

Perhaps the most important point I would like to make on this topic in keeping consistent with the thesis of this book is that we should fast so as to identify with human suffering. People in this world are starving; therefore, I should eat modestly. People in this world are hungry; therefore, I should fast. Fasting in essence is the opposite of feasting. We feast to celebrate the joys of life; we fast to identify with the harsh realities of life. Too much feasting indicates an unbalanced and unrealistic view of the world. Many of us are in continual feasting mode without even being aware of it. This book has simply been a call to such awareness.

At the time of this writing I have been enjoying perhaps the most blessed season of my life, and I am able to reflect on a period of a few good years that have seen few hardship interruptions. I rejoice in this, but certainly this has not always been the case in my life. I have fasted in the past out of a pressing urgency and necessity to do so because of particular troubling times that had come my way. By fasting again, even now when life is not so hard, I commemorate some of my past negative experiences and keep my mind and heart temperate because of the ups and downs that I know life can bring. Also, I should fast because I yet have a life to live and a future to experience. But perhaps more than that, the reason I should fast is because there are many people in the world who suffer now in the present. In other words, I do not merely fast for personal concerns, growth, and spirituality, but I fast so that I might also take on the burden of others who might be suffering or struggling in life. One of the surest ways to do this is to call a personal fast for a short season where one foregoes palatable pleasure and daily sustenance so that that one might enter into the hardship of another. One might call a personal fast on behalf of a friend, a family member, a larger community, or a world concern, or one might even fast for the burden of a stranger! People who are suffering tend not to have an appetite. Worry, concern, stress, and grief all take away the natural desire to eat, thereby elevating one's awareness of greater issues in life, issues of the heart, soul, mind, and spirit. I have personally observed individuals who are going through a difficult time lose a tremendous amount of weight, and not because they were trying. Once life is restored in a positive way, the weight comes back again as the appetite returns to normal. Fasting can simply be entering into the pathos of another.

In short, we should consider approaching fasting as we should consider approaching eating—with a larger worldview in mind. Although fasting is mentioned rather minimally in the New Testament, it appears at some key junctures, such as when the young Church was launching its first gospel mission to the Gentile world (Acts 13:2) and upon commissioning the first elders of newly established congregations (Acts 14:23). In these contexts, fasting is associated with world mission. When such is brought into consideration, fasting becomes not merely the act of disciplining one's eating, or seeking personal spiritual benefits, but it becomes representative of one's entire way of life, a sort of symbol of Christian faith in action. By virtue of the new nature in Christ, the Christian fasts as a personal reminder that one is tends to be private and individualistic, with street markets being replaced by large stores and public transportation and walking being replaced by automobiles, two to three to a house. We have less interaction with each other and therefore tend to leave each other to fend for ourselves.

THE ROLE OF FOOD AND EATING IN ISRAEL'S LAW CODE

Besides such expectations as hospitality for ancient Israel, they were also commanded to observe a rigorous set of food and dietary laws according to the Law of Moses (Lev 11 and Deut 14). It is quite a complicated list of do's and don'ts that thankfully, for the Christian, have become obsolete with the coming of Christ and his gospel (Mark 7:18–19; Acts 10:9–16). For the Israelite committed to the Mosaic laws in earlier days, the mandatory, careful attention given to food regarded as clean and food regarded as unclean certainly must have added to the difficulty of providing available and edible meals, a concept that is far removed from where most of us are at today when it comes to food.

The actual reason for the dietary restrictions for ancient Israel has been a matter of debate and speculation. Perhaps they were arbitrary,[7] given for no other reason than simply to test Israel's obedience. Such an approach, although supported by some of the leading rabbis, has little to commend it.

Perhaps the distinctions were designed to keep Israel separate from pagan religious practices.[8] Certain cultic rituals practiced by heathen nations used particular animals in their worship—for instance the pig, which was very much banned from Israelite menus. Yet other animals, such as the bull, were commonly used in Egyptian and Canaanite worship but considered acceptable and clean as a Levitical altar sacrifice for the

7. Wolf, *An Introduction to the Old Testament Pentateuch*, 176.
8. Ibid., 176.

Hebrews. There appears to be no real rhyme or reason if one tries to press the point of religious distinction being the main purpose of the clean and unclean animal laws.

A third suggestion is that the food laws, and the purity and cleanliness associated with them, were a matter of wholeness or normality.[9] That is, any creature with a deviation from normality within a particular animal class rendered that creature unclean. Take, for instance, a flying insect that also walked on all six legs. The creature might exhibit confusion between the bird realm and the insect realm and therefore could not be considered a pure member of any particular class. The thinking is that just as the priests had to be free from any physical deformity (Lev 21:17–21), so also any deviation from normality within a particular animal class rendered that member unclean. This is a minority view among scholars.

A fourth view is that the clean and unclean animal distinctions were made for health and hygienic reasons.[10] Unclean animals were often the carriers of disease. Pigs carried several parasitic organisms that could cause serious infection. Most of the unclean birds preyed on carrion and could cause infection. Fish without scales often fed on sewage and carried dangerous bacteria. Even other nations in the Ancient Near East considered such food unacceptable. By observing the clean and unclean distinction, the Hebrews would help themselves stay clear of the diseases of Egypt (Exod 15:26) and would by and large stay free from parasites and worms in order to develop healthy conditions in which to live as they approached their own land of promise. The clean animals' more vegetarian diet meant that they would be less likely to transmit infections than animals that ate rapidly decaying flesh in such a hot climate. The Hebrew diet was generally good for health, as can be seen in Daniel when he and his friends did not allow themselves to be forced into a Babylonian

9. Ibid., 177.
10. Ibid., 176.

not to carry anything to excess and is to know when to draw the line as far as bodily appetites are concerned.[1]

Many other things could be said on the topic of fasting, which is beyond the scope of this book. One should of course discuss one's personal health and fasting options with a qualified physician before taking on such asceticism. Our discussion has been about the theological side of fasting. There is much to know about the health benefits of fasting as well. According to Dr. Don Colbert, "Fasting is the safest and best way to heal the body from degenerative diseases caused by being overfed with the wrong nutrition."[2] He also states:

> Our nation is suffering an epidemic of degenerative diseases and death that is caused by excess-plain and simple. We have eaten too much sugar, too much fat, too many empty calories and far too much processed, devitalized food.[3]

Or again:

> More than anything else, fasting is a dynamic key to cleansing your body from a lifetime collection of toxins, reversing over-nourishment and the diseases it brings and ensuring a wonderful future of renewed energy, vitality, longevity and blessed health.[4]

A worthy theological approach to food, eating, diet, and weight control will incorporate some mode of fasting into one's lifestyle, along with the other things that we have been attempting to say in this book.

It is quite possible, and quite likely, that many of us might consider ourselves to being doing just fine when it comes to

1. Smith, *Fasting: A Neglected Discipline*, 16.
2. Colbert, *Toxic Relief*, 45.
3. Ibid, 45.
4. Ibid, 39.

matters of physical indulgence. After all, if we are not addicted to tobacco, drugs, alcohol, pornography, or gambling, we might consider ourselves to be well above reproach. This might be true to some degree. However, this book has contended that most of us could and should be doing far better in matters of food over-indulgence and abuse. Eating consists of moral and ethical virtues, as do the matters of tobacco, alcohol, and drug usage. We may regard others who are ensnared in such vice with contempt yet not be aware that we ourselves just might be gluttonous, carnal, and spiritually weak when it comes to our approach to food. It is not only the overweight person who can be an abuser of food!

Since we have just mentioned alcohol, it might be useful to make a few comments about it, since it too concerns the matter of food and drink we put in our bodies. The Bible no doubt condemns drunkenness (e.g., 1 Cor 6:10). However, it is unreasonable to conclude elsewhere in the Bible that putting alcohol into the body in any given amount or context is an unqualified sin (e.g., 1 Tim 5:23). So then, what to do? For starters, cultures are different. European culture generally incorporates social drinking more readily than American culture, and this can be seen even in the Christian Church. My European Christian friends would hardly give a second thought to having a modest drink on any given occasion, whereas many of my American Christian friends would not even consider such an action. The issue might best be left to individual conviction, consideration, and context, perhaps similarly to the food sacrificed to idols issue discussed by Paul in Romans 14 and 1 Corinthians 8 and following.

However, in light of the larger thesis contended for in this book, the choice to drink alcohol should be made with the same temperance, modesty, and worldview in mind that should be present when it comes to food. Because much of the world suffers and goes without basic provisions, one should not over-indulge in strong drink, whether it is celebratory, social, or full-blown inebriation. Also, when one considers the social problems that oftentimes have alcohol abuse at the root (broken homes, vehicular accidents, crime, etc.), one should desire to be very cautious about partaking. Again, in quoting Saint Paul one more time, we are simply asking, "Whether you eat or drink, or whatever you do, do everything for the glory of God" (1 Cor 10:31). Think before you eat or drink! We should exercise restraint in judging one another in these matters, although the superior biblical model appears to be the abstinence of those like Samson, who unfortunately strayed from his Nazarite vows (Judg 13), and especially John the Baptist (Luke 1:15). Their abstinence from alcohol was related to the intensity of their divine call and mission. The more we live, eat, and drink with a world awareness, the less we desire to seek fleshly gratification of any variety.

Another issue to take into consideration in regard to food, eating, diet, and weight control from a theological vantage point is the matter of vegetarianism. Just as we briefly asked the question about whether alcohol can be consumed from a biblical perspective, we now ask the question about whether animals should be consumed from a biblical perspective. Once again, this is an issue that extends far beyond the reach of the main concern of this book.[5] However, choosing to eat meat, as most of us do, has some theological considerations. Consider, for instance, that the initial divine plan appears to have been for humankind to have eaten vegetation only (Gen 1:11–12, 29). The fact that the living creatures of the earth shared the same day of creation as humankind, day six, might itself be a theological clue that such animals should be treated with a certain amount of respect by humans. It is a curiosity that fish and fowl, which incidentally are generally better meat from a dietary standpoint than land creatures, do not share the same day of creation as human beings.

Vegetation was created as food for the animals as well (Gen 1:30). However, it must be noted that humankind was clearly

5. I would once again recommend Michael Pollan's extensive treatment of the topic in chapter 17 of *The Omnivore's Dilemma.*

given rule and dominion over the animal kingdom (Gen 1:26–28). And although humans lived in harmony with all manners of creature initially, this would distinctively change after the sin in the Garden of Eden and the Noahic flood (Gen 9:1–3). Meat was now added to the menu, which in fact might have been a gift for struggling humanity who had to labor to bring forth food from the earth because of the curse (Gen 3:17–19). The horror of the flood was so great that it appears that God, who did not want to commit such an act again, was reaching out to humanity to help them to start over (Gen 9:8–17). Increased food opportunities might have been one way to do so.

In brief, humans hold a special and unique place as being created in the very image of God, unlike any other created thing, animate or inanimate. God has given both vegetation and the animal world for humans to eat. There should be freedom in this matter. However, when one keeps in mind that the time period before the pre-Edenic sinful action was a period of peaceful co-existence between man and beast and that the prophetic vision is for just such a restoration (Isa 11:6, 8), one concludes that harmony with animals is to be sought as much as possible.[6] Now I have no intention of attempting to shake hands with a bear or swim with a shark, but I do think that eating less meat is, once again, a matter of temperance. Just as in the ancient world meat was a luxury item, so also it is today for the less fortunate around the globe. To eat much meat is to be a glutton. To be a meat and potatoes eater almost exclusively is to eat amiss. We could also go into a lengthy discussion of the dangers of over-consumption of especially red meat from a health standpoint, but that is to be left to other books and experts in the field of diet and nutrition.

My personal conclusion, and what I would like to put into practice in matters of food and diet, is to eat food with the theological mindset I have contended for in this book. This includes ingesting minimal amounts of alcohol, if any, and perhaps for

6. Ibid., 308.

reasons not even mentioned here. It also includes eating meat in moderation, with those animals that swim or fly taking precedence over walking, creeping, or crawling creatures. In other words, eat more fish and fowl and less red meat. Overall, the theological approach to food, eating, diet, and weight control contended for in this book will guide one into a fuller spiritual, emotional, psychological, and even physical life, a life that thinks far beyond self and personal gratification, a life that always has God and others in mind.

Appendix

The Ten Commandments of Eating

THERE IS an old adage that states, "A man digs his own grave with his fork and his knife." This saying needs little commentary. Learning to think differently about food can be a life-altering, and perhaps even a life-saving, experience. Instead of asking the common question, "What is there to eat?" we should learn to ask, "Why is it we eat?" This book has attempted to answer this question in part, at least in a theological sense. Since we are thinking theologically about food, perhaps it would be helpful to have a *ten commandments* of eating. It would be very useful to put these to memory and then apply them whenever we are preparing to eat.

The first commandment of eating should be, "Think before you eat." Learning to slow down and be deliberate about our food intake is first a necessary step toward changing our eating habits for the better. I have employed this "commandment" on numerous occasions and have discovered it to be a great help. The second commandment of eating is assonantly close, "Thank before you eat." Learning to give God praise for the nourishment and pleasure of food will create within us a less self-centered approach to the table. The third commandment is, "Choose health over pleasure" when eating. Conscious food choices need to be made on a daily basis. Although we should at times treat ourselves, this should not be the norm or the rule. Commandment number four is, "Take small portions." We must train ourselves in this. It could be of help to use smaller plates or to always think of a meal when dining out as requiring a doggy bag so that one meal actually becomes two. The fifth commandment is like the fourth, "Take one serving." Again, as long as we always have the first commandment of eating in our minds, we can implement a new lifestyle of not going back for seconds, thirds, and hopefully I don't have to say it, fourths.

Eating commandment number six is, "Eat slowly." This is good for all-around digestion, social etiquette, and helping us to eat less. The seventh commandment of eating is, "Chew often." This is like the previous commandment; it will cause us to eat more slowly and aid our digestive process. Commandment number eight is, "Stop eating slightly before getting full." The brain catches up with the stomach oftentimes later than it should. We don't realize that we have actually eaten enough, and therefore, we need to deliberately stop eating what would appear to be to us prematurely. This might mean leaving food on the plate from time to time, although I certainly don't encourage waste. Eating commandment number nine is, "Hunger pangs are good." Now I do not mean that this is true for people in the world who are genuinely starving. But for most us who rarely experience hunger pangs because of an abundance of food, a hunger pang more often than not is a good sign that we are disciplining our body and being more temperate in matters of eating. Finally, the tenth commandment in our special list is, "Prefer others when eating." This has been a main tenet of this book. This might mean that we let others in the food line before us, or that we seek table fellowship with others. It might mean that we share our food or practice hospitality. Or it might mean that we don't stare at other people's food. The list can go on and on, but the main point is that we train ourselves to think differently about food and the act of eating, with a theological perspective at the forefront. Here is a list of the ten commandments of eating:

1. You shall think before you eat.

2. You shall thank before you eat.

3. You shall choose health over pleasure.

4. You shall take small portions.

5. You shall take one serving.

6. You shall eat slowly.

7. You shall chew often.

8. You shall stop eating slightly before getting full.

9. You shall welcome hunger pangs.

10. You shall show preference to others when eating.

Put these to memory, and practice them right away. May your theological approach to eating, diet, and weight control bring you into a fuller and healthier spiritual, emotional, psychological, and physical life.[1]

1. For further reading on this topic of food, God, and spirituality, see Jung, *Food for Life*.

Bibliography

Aquinas, Saint Thomas. *Summa Theologiae: A Concise Translation*. Translated by Timothy McDermott. Allen, Texas: Christian Classics, 1991.

Aristotle. *The Nicomachean Ethics*. Translated by David Ross. New York: Oxford University Press, 1998.

Augustine. *Basic Writings (Volume I-Confessions & Twelve Treatises)*, edited by Whitney J. Oates. Grand Rapids, Michigan: Baker Book House, reprinted 1992.

Barth, Markus. *Rediscovering the Lord's Supper*. Atlanta, Georgia: John Knox Press, 1988.

Belasco, Warren J. *Meals to Come: A History of the Future of Food*. Berkeley, California: University of California Press, 2006.

Bowden, John. *Who's Who in Theology*. London: SCM Press, 1990.

Buford, Bill. *Heat: an Amateur's Adventures as Kitchen Slave, Line Cook, Pasta-Maker, and Apprentice to a Dante-Quoting Butcher in Tuscany*. New York: Alfred A. Knopf, 2006.

Carson, D.A. "Matthew." In *The Expositor's Bible Commentary (volume 8)*, edited by Frank E. Gaebelein. Grand Rapids, Michigan: Zondervan Publishing House, 1984.

Cochrane, Arthur. *Eating and Drinking with Jesus: An Ethical and Biblical Inquiry*. Philadelphia, Pennsylvania: Westminster Press, 1974.

Colbert, Don. *Toxic Relief*. Lake Mary, Florida: Siloam Press, 1979.

Feeley-Harnik, Gillian. *The Lord's Table: The Meaning of Food in Early Judaism and Christianity*. Washington DC: Smithsonian Institution Press, 1981.

Frick, Frank S. *A Journey Through the Hebrew Scriptures*. Belmont, California: Thomson/Wadsworth, 2003.

Gower, Ralph. *The New Manners and Customs of Bible Times*. Chicago: Moody Press, 1987.

Gunkel, Hermann. *Genesis (A Commentary)*. Translated by John Scullion. Minneapolis, Minnesota: Augsburg Publishing House, 1981.

Hafer, Tom P. *Faith & Fitness (Diet and Exercise for a Better World)*. Minneapolis, Minnesota: Augsburg Books, 2007.

Halliday, Judy and Arthur, *Thin Again: A Biblical Approach to Food, Eating, and Weight Management*. Grand Rapids, Michigan: Fleming H. Revell A Division of Baker Book House Co, 1994.

Harris, R. Laird. "Leviticus." In *The Expositor's Bible Commentary (volume 2)*, edited by Frank E. Gaebelein. Grand Rapids, Michigan: Zondervan Publishing House, 1990.

Jung, Shannon. *Food for Life: The Spirituality and Ethics of Eating*. Minneapolis, Minnesota: Augsburg Fortress Press, 2004.

Lewis, C.S. *The Screwtape Letters*. New York: The Macmillan Company, 1946.

Logue, A.W. *The Psychology of Eating and Drinking: An Introduction*, 2nd edition. New York: W.H. Freeman and Company, 1986.

Mason, Jim, and Singer, Peter. *The Way We Eat: Why Our Food Choices Matter*. Emmaus, Pennsylvania: Rodale Press, 2006.

Morris, Leon. "1 Corinthians." In *Tyndale New Testament Commentaries (volume 7)*, revised edition. Grand Rapids, Michigan: William B. Eerdmans Publishing Company, 1993.

Nestle, Marion. *What to Eat*. New York: North Point Press, 2006.

Nouwen, Henri J.M. *With Burning Hearts: A Meditation on the Eucharistic Life*. Mary-Knoll, New York: Orbis Books, 1994.

Pleij, Herman. *Dreaming of Cockaigne*. Translated by Diane Webb. New York: Columbia University Press, 2001.

Pollan, Michael. *In Defense of Food: An Eater's Manifesto*. New York: The Penguin Press, 2008.

Pollan, Michael. *The Omnivore's Dilemma: A Natural History of Four Meals*. New York: Penguin Books, 2006.

Prose, Francine. *Gluttony*. New York: Oxford University Press, 2003.

Shaw, Teresa M. *The Burden of the Flesh: Fasting and Sexuality in Early Christianity*. Minneapolis, Minnesota: Fortress Press, 1998.

Smith, David R. *Fasting: A Neglected Discipline*. Fort Washington, Pennsylvania: Christian Literature Crusade, 1954.

Smith, Gordon T. *A Holy Meal: The Lord's Supper in the Life of the Church*. Grand Rapids, Michigan: Baker Academic, 2005.

St. John of the Cross. *Dark Night of the Soul.* Translated by Allison Peers. Garden City, New York: Doubleday, 1959.

Von Rad, Gerhard. *Genesis (A Commentary).* Translated by John Marks. Philadelphia, Pennsylvania: The Westminster Press, 1956.

Wessel, Walter W. "Mark." In *The Expositor's Bible Commentary (volume 8)*, edited by Frank E. Gaebelein. Grand Rapids, Michigan: Zondervan Publishing House, 1984.

Westermann, Claus. *Genesis 12–36 (A Commentary).* Translated by John Scullion. Minneapolis, Minnesota: Augsburg Publishing House, 1981.

Wolf, Herbert. *An Introduction to the Old Testament Pentateuch.* Chicago: Moody Press, 1991.

Wright, Tom. *The Meal Jesus Gave Us: Understanding Holy Communion.* London: John Knox Press, 1999.